# The Ovum's Code

Michael George

ISBN-13: 979-8-224-39719-8

# DEDICATION

To my family and friends,

This book is a tribute to you—my anchors, companions, and guides through the twists and turns of life. Some of you are still by my side, offering unwavering support. Some have taken different paths, but your impact endures. And to those who are no longer here, your influence remains alive in the fabric of my being. Thank you for shaping the person I am today.

With heartfelt appreciation,

Michael George

# INTRODUCTION

Embarking on an exploration of diverse dimensions of human experience, this collection spans an array of thought-provoking topics, delving into the intricacies of life, consciousness, and purpose. From an examination of societal norms to an inquiry into the mysteries of our existence, each chapter weaves a unique narrative. It starts with the perspective of a newborn entering this world, exploring innocent viewpoints, and then gradually shifts to the nuanced perspectives of adulthood, contributing to a collective journey through the depths of human understanding.

As we navigate through these diverse chapters, a recurring thread surfaces—a call for heightened consciousness. From unraveling the complexities of negative work energies to contemplating humanity's salvation through evolved consciousness, there is a shared emphasis on self-awareness, enlightenment, and the pursuit of a more profound understanding that transcends societal confines.

The collection traverses the paradoxes of modern life, from illusions of love in the age of streaming to the distortions of reality within the realms of social media. Amid these paradoxes, a consistent theme emerges—an invitation to break free from constraints, whether mental, societal, or self-imposed.

Each chapter beckons individuals to venture into the realms of consciousness, societal paradigms, and the mysteries that shape our shared human journey. As we commence this exploration, the overarching question, "Why Are We Here on Earth?" stands as an enduring invitation to continue the quest for meaning, understanding, and enlightenment along the intricate path of human existence.

MICHAEL GEORGE

# CONTENTS

# ABOUT THE AUTHOR

Michael George is a seasoned professional with over two decades in the business industry, leaving an indelible mark on software engineering and biotechnology globally. Originally from Brazil, Michael spent his formative years growing up in Washington DC, navigating its cultural landscape before finally settling in Los Angeles, California. A proponent of personal development, he extends his expertise to life coaching, inspiring the next generation through seminars and individual guidance. His commitment to philanthropy is evident in regular donations and active participation in charitable causes. Beyond his corporate prowess, Michael is a versatile musician proficient in multiple instruments and music notation, with a background in Jazz and Classical music. A dedicated reader and writer, his love for literature shines in his book,
The Ovum's Code, where he seamlessly intertwines a collective journey through the depths of human understanding, inviting readers to question, ponder, and explore the profound dimensions of existence.

MICHAEL GEORGE

x

# 1  THE ARRIVAL

Alright, folks, picture this: I'm here, popping my eyes open for the first time, stuck in this pint-sized body that seems to have its own agenda. I'm looking around, desperately trying to make sense of this cosmic circus I've been thrust into. Colors are flashing everywhere, like a rave party, and communication? Well, I'm just a baby genius; what did you expect?

The world looks like it had a paint explosion, and I'm here feeling like an extraterrestrial tourist with a VIP pass to the weirdest show in the galaxy. And let's not even talk about the amazing lady. She's got this magical wand, and every time she inserts it in my mouth, voila! A sip of nourishing celestial liquid, unexpectedly delightful. It's like the cosmos crafting its own smoothie.

Fast forward a couple of hours into this since my arrival, and I've cracked the code. Cry, and they come running. Genius, right? Now, let's dive into the glorious absurdity of waking up in a world where no one knows the rules, and we'll end up taking life advice from people who are just as clueless. Buckle up, because this is gonna be one incredible ride.

## 2  EARLY PERSPECTIVES OF LIFE AND DEATH

And there she goes again, hollering my name like we're about to embark on a mission to save the world. "Michael, grab your bags, you're late for school!" Sound familiar? Yeah, I bet you've been on the receiving end of a similar wake-up call.

So, here I am, pondering the cosmic question: Is this why you, oh mysterious being from the other realm, sent me here for? To experience a life where I've got zero freedom and a boss lady who's got a black belt in bossing people around, all day, every day? At this point, I'm just scratching the surface of what seems like an endless journey filled with bosses queuing up, ready to give me orders. And the kicker? I have absolutely no clue that freedom is playing hide and seek somewhere in the distant future. The only thought on my mind? "Can't wait to hit 18, like that's gonna be my golden ticket to a boss-free paradise." Oh, the naivety of youth!

At the break of the afternoon, here she is, belting out questions and insults over the phone, and I'm standing there coping with only one side of the story, sipping my imaginary tea, pretending to care. Sounds familiar, right? I figure it's the dude who chauffeurs me around every weekend on the other side of the line.

Now, let's take a detour down memory lane. I'm chilling with a buddy who lost both parents before even doing the diaper dance. I ask, "You good?" He hits me with, "It's okay now," and we both share a laugh. Classic coping mechanism, right? So, I throw in my two cents, "Hey, I got two parents; you want 'em?" We crack up because, let's face it, life's a lot of fun. We'll circle back to my pal in a bit. Don't worry; he's got his own spot in this cosmic tale.

Back to the phone call soap opera— they're still at it, and just when things get interesting, Aunt Interruption strolls in, hijacks the conversation, and drops the funeral bomb. "Are you going?" she asks. "Yes, we are," she says, throwing in that royal "we" like I'm part of some funeral field trip. Oh, and by the way, what's a funeral? No one tells me anything; they just toss toys my way like life's a perpetual Toys 'R' Us spree. Off we go to the funeral, and as we arrive, I'm thinking, "Wow, this is creepy!" Sure, I've seen a spooky movie or two, but it's the first time I've encountered a gathering of dead folks, like they're having a weird family reunion at Toys 'R' Us. Sorry, but that's what it looked like to my little eyes — a reunion of the dead in the toy kingdom. Sounds morbid, but to my pint-sized brain, it's the undead's idea of a playdate. And hey, ever wonder if funerals are only creepy because we make 'em that way? We're taught that death is the ultimate horror show, so let's throw a party so forgettable that you'll be scared to visit a graveyard again. It's just like how grown-ups preach about marriage being eternal, Santa being an annual gift dispenser, and, of course, that we're the center of the universe. Ah, childhood, where sarcasm is the secret language, and everything is one big cosmic joke.

# 3  PARENTING ECHOING ACROSS GENERATIONS

Fast forward to the ripe age of 16, and guess who's become my live-in chauffeur? Yep, you got it—good old dad, the same guy who used to pick me up on weekends. Now, here's the kicker: he was never a chauffeur by trade, but did look like one at the time. No, sir. At this point, he's a wealthy, highly-educated, and, might I add, egoistic dude. His priorities? Well, they revolve more around his own indulgences than anything else. But hey, considering the wild ride I've had so far, who can blame him?

Here I am, sharing the mansion with him and his third wife. Hold on, rewind a bit; she's been around for about 14 years now, so not exactly a newcomer. I'm tempted to hop into a time machine and ask my old buddy if he's still on the lookout for parents because, let me tell you, I've got a trio, and none of them are what you'd call "normal." But then again, who is normal, especially when they're from good old Earth?

Diving back into my teenage years talk, the so-called "best years of my life." Why? Because I'm blissfully ignorant of what lies ahead. My head, however, has been a dumping ground for all sorts of junk, courtesy of the clueless people of this world and the ones before them. Picture this: if you could gather all the 16-year-old teenagers from around the globe and analyze the data in their heads, you'd see a mishmash of experiences that aren't exactly unique. They're influenced by everything around them—people, things, you name it.

Now, throw in another group, say, in their 30s or 40s. Line them up against the teens and ask them to spot the differences. The 30-somethings might think they've got it all figured out, having been around the block longer. But the truth? They're just carrying a load of programmed experiences, shaped by other means, time, and space. Why does this matter? Because it paves the way for everything you want to be and achieve in life.

Pay close attention, and you'll realize—you're not making choices in your best interest. You're often following a script written by the traumas, experiences, and beliefs of those around you. Life, in general, molds itself for you, and you're letting it happen. To regain control, you've got to identify all the stuff that's been dumped into you, messing with your decisions and, in many cases, not exactly healthy for you.

Let me throw an example your way—a mother, deeply rooted in religion, eager to plant her ideas in your head simply because grandma did the same for her. See how these things get passed down from generation to generation, affecting who you are today? There's a common thread in all of this—it's a lingering state of consciousness called fear. But fear? We'll save that chat for later, exploring how it plays a starring role in shaping the outcome of your life.

# 4 RETHINKING MARRIAGE AND EMBRACING REALISM

Let's fast-forward this journey again in a Time Machine, landing in my mid-30s. As an accomplished professional who has weathered the storm of a divorce, I now find myself in the company of a spirited woman in her mid-20s, marking a new chapter in my life.

Reflecting on the aftermath of my divorce, I chose not to attribute blame, opting for a more detached perspective on what is commonly perceived as a stressful experience. I observe that people often struggle to confront the reality of marriage, clinging to it even as relationships naturally evolve. The societal model ingrained in our minds, coupled with the fear of the unknown, frequently compels individuals to persevere through circumstances that may be better left behind.

Challenging the traditional marriage vows, particularly, the phrase "until death do us part," I view it as an unrealistic and fear-inducing notion. I suggest a more honest expression, such as "I hope you make it through all the challenges" or a simple "I wish you both luck." My argument revolves around the acknowledgment of human fallibility and the understanding that death, in the grand scheme, unites us all eventually.

I want to clarify that I'm not discouraging marriage outright. Instead, I advocate for a realistic approach, urging individuals to align their expectations with what their partners can genuinely endure. This, I believe, can foster a relationship unburdened by unrealistic ideals and free from unnecessary fears.

As the narrative unfolds, I promise to delve into the fear aspect, assuring you that these thoughts will seamlessly come together, providing a comprehensive and coherent perspective. The anticipation builds, leaving you eager to uncover the deeper insights I have in store.

Now heading back in time, riding shotgun with Doc in the DeLorean, I find myself at 18, utterly clueless about life. Freshly parted from my high school sweetheart, that moment of young love that feels boundless. At 18, the world tosses challenges at you without a rulebook, and everyone seems eager to offer advice on moving on to bigger and better things. However, deep down, it's hard to take their guidance to heart because, in my own judgment, I felt they didn't necessarily know any better.

Adding to the mix, my dad's nudging me toward a military career, a dream my mom harbored for a long time. She envisioned me following in my father's Air Force footsteps – a path he had retired from by then. Yet, my heartbeat to a different tune; I aspired to be a musician, and in the end, I pursued neither. Defying expectations, I said, "Screw everybody, I'm going to college." My decision was driven by a desire to make practical choices, charting a course toward the freedom I yearned for.

Now, you might wonder, "Why not pursue music since that's what you truly wanted?" Well, hop in the DeLorean, revisit that moment, and ask me then.

Was fear a factor? Who's to say? Almost 99.9% of the time, our choices are tinged with the influence of fear. And that's precisely what we're about to explore next.

## 5  JOURNEY THROUGH SENSES: EMOTIONS, LOVE, AND THE UNSEEN FORCES

It's finally time to delve into the realm of fear. Before we dig into its complexities, let's examine a few senses that are typically considered receptive due to their tangible, physical nature. We often think about our five senses—like touch and smell—when considering what we can feel. These senses deal with concrete, tangible things. When scientists discuss it, they focus on what's observable and touchable. But what about that 'sixth sense' we often talk about? Well, in this book, we'll explore it. It's not as mysterious as we might believe; in fact, it's more physical than we realize.

Let's consider an analogy: the wind. It's intangible, much like the elusive nature of love. Our awareness of the wind comes from its interaction with a receptive system, specifically the sense of touch.

Now, transitioning from the exploration of senses and emotions, let's journey back to my 25-year-old self, navigating the past intricacies of living with someone in a four-year relationship. In those days, she was nothing short of extraordinary. The purity of love in youth shielded us from many complexities. However, the reality of two unique individuals attempting to build a life together introduced its own set of distinctive challenges.

Picture a typical Saturday afternoon – we're settled in to watch a movie. She leans towards romance, I lean towards action. The ensuing debate, lasting a good 30 minutes, inevitably leads to the romantic choice. The movie goes on, love blossoms, ends, and soon hunger calls. Now, a dispute over ordering Chinese or grabbing burgers takes another 30 minutes, culminating in a compromise for Chinese cuisine – her choice as the winner once again.

Post-dinner, I lose myself in the world of Xbox, immersing in a multiplayer session of Call of Duty with a buddy who, coincidentally, is also navigating the complexities of cohabitation. My focus is so intense that her frustration with my gaming addiction takes me by surprise. "Again? Can't you play this some other time?" she exclaims. The argument continues, my attention fixated on the gaming world, strategizing with my friend about in-game tactics.

She interrupts the gaming session three times in two hours. At this age, relationships feel akin to a game of Chess—moves and countermoves played out without full comprehension. She wins in choosing the movie (moving the Knight) and deciding on Chinese food (by moving the Bishop). In return, I immerse myself in a marathon gaming session, moving my Queen. But, as in Chess, the game isn't over until you checkmate the King.

In her fourth visit to the living room, she dealt a decisive blow by pulling the plug on the console—it's checkmate. I had a 50-kill streak with built-up momentum in this online multiplayer gaming session, something our friends online would consider a crime if suddenly interrupted. It felt like dropping an atomic bomb on our prolonged dispute, as if we were concluding a global war of our own. What followed were intense arguments that reached a boiling point when, in a moment of frustration, I impulsively tossed my joystick towards the kitchen, hitting a vase with a plant she had recently purchased for the house. In return, she responded with broken plates and a demand for me to do the dishes right before locking herself in the room. Forty-five minutes of tense silence later, we called a truce.

Curious about the connection between two romantic, in-love savages and the understanding of fear? We'll unravel that mystery shortly. But first, let's explore a clear understanding of what feelings entail. We'll probe into the integration of emotions into the physical and tangible world before reaching our destination in the ongoing exploration of this book.

Amidst the chaos, a symphony of emotions echoes through the walls: my frustration over the dinner choice, her joy in getting her way, my pleasure in gaming, and her frustration at not getting what she wanted. Sensory experiences of hearing, smelling, tasting, touch, and sight intertwine with intangible emotions and energies.

We often perceive these emotions and energies as intangible, much like the wind. But could they possess a physical receptor that escapes our perception? Perhaps, unnoticed, they quietly reshape life in so many ways.

In the present, our understanding of sensory experiences is typically limited to the well-known five: hearing, smell, taste, touch, and vision. This understanding is supported by the presence of physical receptors in the process of perception. However, we often use phrases like "it was like a punch in the face" to describe emotional experiences. This comparison opens the door to the idea that the physical pain of a punch might mirror the emotional pain of betrayal or heartbreak. Could it be that these conscious states are more tangible than our conventional understanding suggests? Consider the time needed for healing after a physical punch – is it so different from the time needed to heal after a breakup or betrayal? If the answer is a resounding yes, then perhaps we've been underestimating the physical nature of intuitions, emotions, and feelings. The physical power in our sixth sense.

Picture a boxing match as a dynamic dance, where opponents strategically unleash a flurry of punches, targeting various parts of their adversary's body. Now, envision a verbal confrontation, where two individuals throw a combination of words, ultimately leading to one's emotional defeat. The crux lies in the realization that victory doesn't always require a physical punch; emotions might possess a profound physicality that surpasses our conventional understanding. Although invisible like the wind, emotions may have a tangible presence—a dimension waiting for scientific validation.

The wind, though unseen, is air in motion, felt against our skin. Similarly, acts of love or betrayal from others often manifest physically within us. Consider the acknowledgment of betrayal, which can induce a chilling sensation down our throat—an ephemeral pain that fades away if the betrayal is proven untrue. This departure of pain leaves behind a sense of healing that spreads through our body. The analogy to wounds and their intensity further emphasizes that this emotional experience can either penetrate deeply or reveal itself as merely a superficial scratch in intensity. Neurochemical changes, particularly in serotonin and dopamine levels, further underscore the physical nature of emotions.

Now, how does this connect to fear? Fear, much like the emotions we've explored, is woven into this intricate web. If emotions indeed possess a physical reality, they exert a colossal influence on our human experience. Reflecting on a heated argument with my girlfriend, it unleashed a cascade of emotional elements, reshaping what could have been a serene Saturday afternoon. Invoking emotions such as control, desire, selfishness, and the fear of letting go led to a disastrous outcome—with a broken joystick and shattered plates. We feared releasing our grip, turning a potentially beautiful afternoon into chaos. As we delve deeper, we will uncover more facets of fear and other emotions, unraveling their profound impact on our physical world. This journey illuminates the tangible nature of emotions, challenging some of our established beliefs.

Now, let's ponder emotions we acknowledge, assigning names to them, yet confining them to the realms of psychological and cognitive perspectives. What about desires, pride, anger, or joy? Where do these emotions originate? Are they a form of energy? Are they receptive? They undeniably resemble a sensory system, playing a substantial role in our physical state when emitted or received. Should we limit them to the realms of psychology and cognition, or should we venture beyond these mystical states to unravel their potential as keys to our salvation or our peril if left unattended?

As we ponder the tangible nature of emotions and their profound impact on our human experience, we find ourselves at the crossroads of understanding the intricate web that binds our emotional and physical realms. Having explored the sensory aspects of emotions, we now turn our gaze toward challenging another fascinating facet of human nature—our inherent tendency to pull back against imposed limits.

# 6  HUMAN POTENTIAL UNLEASHED

Human nature often inclines towards setting limits, establishing boundaries that delineate the extent of our capabilities. If you were to ask an individual whether they could soar through the sky unaided, the notion might be dismissed as absurd or even delusional. This inclination to circumscribe our potential is deeply ingrained.

Consider the realm of sports. In 1936, Joe Fortenberry accomplished the first dunk in basketball, a feat that, at the time, may have seemed the pinnacle of human leaping ability. Fast forward to the present, and men can now execute dunks from the free throw line, pushing the boundaries of what was once thought possible.

Reflecting on the track and field legacy, Carl Lewis carved his name into history in 1983 as the first man to break the 10-second barrier in the 100-meter dash at low altitude, a feat recorded on an automatic timing clock. Lewis's achievement marked a pivotal moment in the sport. Fast forward nearly two decades, and the Jamaican sprinter Usain Bolt eclipsed the 100-meter milestone with remarkable speed. In 2009, Bolt shattered the all-time record, crossing the finish line with noteworthy acceleration, a mere over 0.20 seconds faster. Extrapolating from this progression, one might speculate, without delving into the nuances of technological advancements, biological factors, or the intricacies of the sport, that a man could conceivably run 100 meters in 7.5 seconds by the year 2228 and perhaps even dip below 6 seconds by 2388. This is a practical estimate based on historical progress and the breaking of barriers in human evolution.

At first glance, these projections may elicit incredulity. Humans tend to dismiss such notions as fantastical, almost instinctively resistant to embracing the seemingly impossible. Yet, this skepticism is precisely the point. As a species, we often impose limits on ourselves until someone, somewhere, defies the conventional wisdom, proving that what was once deemed unattainable is, in fact, within reach. It prompts us to question why we are so quick to react to the achievements of others, especially when the inherent nature of humanity is one of boundless potential.

The crux of the matter lies in challenging these preconceived limitations. If we can collectively grasp the concept of our innate limitlessness, unshackling ourselves from the constraints of doubt and skepticism, we have the power to propel the evolution of our species at an unprecedented pace. The key lies in embracing the limitless nature of the human spirit and daring to push the boundaries of what we believe is achievable.

The overarching message is to encourage us to discard limiting beliefs and embrace the demonstrated truth that humans have repeatedly shown to be boundless in the acquisition of infinite knowledge.

# 7  A 24-HOUR PAUSE IN THE STREAM OF THOUGHTS

Let's embark on an exploration, an experiment that delves into the duality of your existence—the current you and the envisioned version of yourself. Picture the first iteration, the you of today, a persona entangled in a web of ceaseless thoughts. These thoughts, a dissonance ranging from personal relationships to work-related concerns, ambitions, financial worries, family matters, and the myriad complexities of daily life, collectively shape your state of happiness. They hold the reins, steering the course of your peace of mind.

Now, shift your focus to the second version of yourself, a version where the relentless stream of thoughts is intentionally silenced for a mere 24 hours. In this alternate reality, free from the usual concerns and activities that occupy your mind, imagine the profound tranquility that could ensue. A day of absolute stillness, where the burden of thought is temporarily lifted, leading you into a realm of bliss so serene that the prospect of returning to the incessant mental chatter becomes almost undesirable.

Consider this: which of the two versions do you perceive as the happier? One might argue that achieving such a state in our bustling world is an impossibility, given the external constraints that often dictate our discomfort. However, the reality is quite different. While external influences may appear to play a role in shaping our sense of peace, the true power lies within us. We hold the reins to decide whether these external forces will impact our inner tranquility.

To embody the second version in this experiment, one must practice the art of controlling thoughts. In moments of discomfort, instead of passively absorbing the energies that threaten to plunge us into despair, we must learn to wield the shield of mental strength. This involves countering incoming negative energies with a conversion tool—a tool that reduces concerns to mere specks in the vast universe. Repeat to yourself, "This is nothing; I will just take care of it."

Through consistent application of this technique of filtering your thoughts, especially when confronted with life's obstacles, we train our minds to filter problems to a point where mastery is achieved. Problems cease to be perceived as such; they become as effortless to navigate as the act of breathing. This cultivated sense of constant happiness becomes a guiding force as we traverse the journey of our lifetime. Mastering this internal peace opens the door to unraveling other aspects of life, ultimately leading to success and evolution.

At a pivotal juncture in my life, I found myself entangled in concerns that deviated from my ideals and preoccupied with potential obstacles along my path. Enveloped in constant duress, these worries became formidable barriers obstructing the pursuit of my broader goals. My relentless pursuit of rapid results only yielded a deluge of negative outcomes. Those who hastily navigate their goals often find themselves ensnared by anxiety, stress, and a readiness to forsake their dreams.

Several years later, while addressing an audience at a university in the United States, I underscored a fundamental life lesson. For those aspiring to own a mansion but currently unable to afford one, embrace this wisdom: "If you can't buy the house, acquire it brick by brick, and rest assured, soon you'll have a home." This concept is a sacred elixir for success. Seasoned individuals comprehend the art of patience; they meticulously construct their success over time.

Many yearn to expedite their goals, burdening themselves with undue pressure, often leading to premature surrender. It's analogous to an arduous gym session where exertion is so intense that soreness begets reluctance to continue. The term "bodybuilding" epitomizes this perspective; building, in any form, necessitates time—it is not an overnight endeavor. Make it a habit to cultivate a tranquil mind; it will yield wonders.

# 8  UNDERSTANDING AND DEFUSING NEGATIVE WORK ENERGIES

In the quirky circus of office life, there's always that one special performer, the unrivaled maestro of chaos, the Picasso of peculiarities – your workplace's very own unicorn with extra glitter and confetti. Now, nobody really likes to point fingers, but let's face it, we all have that co-worker who makes dealing with a porcupine seem like a walk in the park. So now that you got this tension of your chest, let's dive further into it.

You found yourself, after a full day of work, returning home only to discover that your mind remains ensnared by the intricacies of a work-related situation? It's a common phenomenon—a mental carryover that extends beyond office hours. You might catch yourself revisiting past discussions or preemptively contemplating scenarios yet to unfold, constructing mental defenses against potential future challenges. In this state, you unknowingly subject yourself to needless suffering over events that have yet to transpire.

Consider a scenario where you grapple with a challenging

colleague at work. Every interaction with this individual carries an anticipation of impending mental strain. The reason lies in the fact that the other person is energetically entrenched in a lower level of consciousness. Their demeanor and energy have the potential to influence your own unless you develop a mechanism to shield yourself from this impact.

For instance, imagine dealing with someone demanding and anxious. Daily interactions with such an individual might gradually induce a sense of anxiety and defensiveness in yourself. This is because lower levels of consciousness, like anger, fear, anxiousness, sadness, worry, and shame, can be contagious if not effectively managed.

By cultivating awareness of these energies in your surroundings, you gain the power to exert control. The key lies in identifying and then releasing these negative energies from your own state of mind. Here's an illustrative example: Picture approaching a barista and inquiring about the availability of soy milk. The response you receive is a sarcastic retort, delivered in a rude manner, implying, "Sorry, but is there a sign indicating that we are a vegan shop?". At this very juncture, you face a pivotal choice: engage in a confrontation, or employ a more nuanced approach by understanding the energetic state of the individual and strategically shaping your response.

In this scenario, you choose the latter. You analyze the negative energy coming from the barista and deliberately filter it, ensuring your own state of consciousness remains unaffected. A well-crafted response, perhaps a light-hearted acknowledgment of their humor followed by a positive comment about something unrelated, such as their hat or purse, becomes your tool to deflect the negative energy. In doing so, you not only shield your own state of mind but also attempt to uplift the barista's consciousness by introducing a positive element, such as kindness, into the interaction. Remember the saying?

"Kill them with Kindness," often recalled, but rarely applied. In this case, you want to uplift them with kindness. The more we embrace this approach of elevating ourselves and others to higher consciousness, the swifter we will witness the gradual disappearance of other negative elements like suffering, sadness, diseases, etc., from mankind's lives. This transformative process marks the emergence of evolved species —an evolution where not only individual minds, but the collective consciousness of humanity is elevated to a state where compassion and positivity reign supreme.

# 9 BREAKING MENTAL CHAINS: FROM SLAVERY TO MASTERY

Recall my buddy, the one who faced parental loss in his early years? Our life trajectories diverged significantly. After numerous years, we reconnected as grown men. He's now a mechanic, toiling away at his cousin's shop, having weathered a few marriages, divorces, and the absence of children. Our reunion took place at a local bar near his residence during one of my town visits, an opportunity to catch up over a couple of beers. Before departing, I handed over my contact details, intending to maintain our connection. Surprisingly, he engaged in frequent messaging, sharing insights into life's twists and turns. Yet, a disconcerting pattern emerged—he seemed persistently dissatisfied, complaining ceaselessly. It was as though nothing ever brought satisfaction, no adventure or life experience was worth relishing.

As our exchanges continued, I discerned a pervasive negativity—a web of discontent and constant depression. His daily narrative echoed this negativity from dawn to dusk, a detrimental loop he seemed unable to break. I intervened, explaining that if he continued to believe that life was miserable every single day, then, undoubtedly, life would unfold as such. His perpetual low state of consciousness hindered him from cultivating higher-quality thoughts, significantly impacting his daily existence. I urged him to release the negative thoughts, but he struggled to break free. This served as a stark reminder—just as one can strive to elevate consciousness to greatness, an unintentional mastery of lower vibrational thinking can also manifest, trapping individuals in a cycle of despair. Unfortunate outcomes, such as depression, suicide, or worse, often result from succumbing to the mastery of degraded thoughts.

One thing to envision in mind is that life works essentially like a blank canvas awaiting its work. The mind acts as the brush, thoughts as the paints, and life as the canvas. Let's embark on a visual exercise: picture yourself in the ocean, attempting to swim back to the shore amidst relentless waves. The struggle intensifies, fatigue sets in, and panic looms. Now, step back from this exercise. Was the experience pleasant? Unlikely. Yet, comprehend that what you just underwent was a mental creation, a narrative you willingly painted. Now, envision the implications when you unwittingly craft negative images of your life daily through your consciousness. Such habitual negativity can lead to devastating outcomes, akin to the scenario in our exercise.

Those demons plaguing your thoughts? You are their creator. The crux lies in realizing that the tapestry of your life is intricately woven by the threads of your perception. The moment you grasp this truth, you gain the power to shape and reclaim control over your existence.

What if the scope of our potential discovery exceeds our current perception? We exhibit a tendency to inflate our knowledge within the confines of this minuscule spectacle we call Earth, arrogantly elevating it beyond the capacity of our own egos. Meanwhile, the expansive universe beckons us to approach our existence with humility, to carve out space for profound growth. Yet, humanity seems fixated on the notion that intelligence on Earth is gauged by navigating a structured school system, accumulating wealth, securing societal success—parameters that supposedly define the pinnacle of human greatness. "How silly are we?" We will expand further upon this point in a later section.

# 10  GOD'S PALETTE WITHIN AN EGGSHELL

During a university seminar in the United States, I was once asked about my belief in God. I responded, expressing my certainty that there is something out there—something more potent and intricately structured than the beliefs we hold here on Earth. This response sparked another question: could I support my statement?

In reply, I offered a simple yet compelling illustration of this unseen power. I pointed to something as ordinary as an egg. Picture this: as you wake up, grab your frypan, and ignite the stove, the moment you crack that egg, take a tiny pause to observe what unfolds. Right before your eyes, you'll witness a kind of magic. Inside, there's a yellowish blob embraced by a white, slimy substance. In essence, it's nothing short of liquid wonder, showcasing the intricacy and power that exist beyond our immediate perceptions.

How, you might ask, could an egg serve as evidence for the existence of a higher power? Instead of merely cracking and consuming an egg, consider allowing it to follow its natural course—a phenomenon we often overlook. This seemingly ordinary object undergoes a magical transformation from a watery blob into a fully functional, almost otherworldly being. It sprouts a beak, a fleshy crest atop its head, dangling lobes under its chin, and a pair of legs complete with claws.

Imagine it this way: if I handed you a cup of water with a mere drop of orange, could you fashion from it a fully functional machine? Perhaps a robot or a computer? The very concept underscores a profound truth—whomever devised the science that turns liquid into a fully functional being is eons ahead of us in terms of intelligence. If you remain unconvinced, consider this challenge: here's a cup of water with a drop of orange—now, construct a machine with it, my friend.

# 11  HUMANITY'S SALVATION THROUGH EVOLVED CONSCIOUSNESS

Scientific principles wield immense influence over the way we navigate our existence today, bestowed upon us by the greatest minds to grace this Earth. These scientific laws illuminate the path that humanity ought to tread to alleviate the lingering sufferings that persist on our planet. Allow me to distill a seemingly simple yet transformative concept: "Once humanity evolves in the faculties we lack and learns to love each other unconditionally, we will then liberate ourselves from the self-inflicted suffering."

Pay heed to the inevitability of this higher level of consciousness essential for the salvation of humankind. Consider a time when misunderstandings or provocations led to swift and deadly retribution. Heads rolled for the slightest transgressions; a mere mockery of the divine could condemn someone to death by stoning, the Brazen Bull—a hollow bronze bull in which a person was placed, and a fire was set underneath—or crucifixion, among other punishments performed by authorities during the Roman and

Persian empires or Ancient Greek eras. These were forms of punishment we now deem inconceivable. Over the years, these acts have evolved, becoming better understood. Despite the ongoing measurement of consciousness progressing with the passage of time, we continue to make strides forward. While we undoubtedly face challenges and suffer, our progress has propelled us into a far better state than ever before.

Yet, it's crucial to acknowledge that this evolutionary journey, spanning from primordial years to the present, has been accompanied by pain, suffering, bloodshed, and death. Any individual who contends that life lacks purpose, that existence holds no meaning, essentially regresses to a primitive state. A closer examination of the intricacies existing on Earth, those not crafted by human hands, reveals profound reasoning in each element.

Scientific contributions, embedded in our biological machinery, serve as catalysts for our evolution. Unfortunately, amidst the chaos of everyday life, this concept often languishes in obscurity as humans divert their attention to frivolities. Envision a world where schools are erected to unravel the mysteries of ourselves, and global education systems are crafted to propel scientific evolution. A utopian vision, perhaps, where life takes a different course. Unfortunately, due to the absence of essential faculties in our current reality, our educational systems are tailored for profit, selfishly driven by greed and survival instincts.

# 12  FROM KINGS TO FOOLS, AN AUTHORITARIAN FOLLY

Upon revisiting the introductory chapters that recount our entry into this world, a discernible preset seems to have been presented to us in that pivotal moment. Imagine stepping into Earth during the epoch of Ancient Rome or amidst the turbulence of our last World War. Each of these distinct eras unveils presets with unique challenges, intricately woven into the societal models they represent. A young man coming of age during World War II grappled with circumstances and challenges distinct from those encountered today. While some might argue for subjectivity based on the specific surroundings of the individual, the overarching complexities and probabilities of those times would still far surpass the challenges of the present day.

Without delving too deeply into this perspective, let's contemplate humanity today and 2000 years ago. Undeniably, these presets offer different outlooks on how humans are shaped at that particular point in time. Upon entering this world, historical presets are already in place, established by those who came before us. As youths, we might refer to them as "Grown-Up Folks." These authorities exert significant influence not only on individuals but on society as a whole. Placed in their roles through various means—be it educational and professional accomplishments or lineage of royalty—these figures possess the power to alter the course of many lives. I'm referring here to kings, queens, politicians, and rulers in general. Most individuals hesitate to challenge the policies and rules proposed by these authorities, as the structural deployment of obedience through the system serves as a means to impose order. Yet, it's worth noting that these orders are, in fact, formulated by other humans—a small group of individuals lacking the same faculties we previously discussed.

In an evolved civilization model, such dynamics wouldn't pose a problem because, in that paradigm, humans know how to do the right thing. Higher levels of consciousness drive advanced civilizations to act justly, preventing them from wrongdoing. However, in our current society, particularly the one we inhabit today, the lack of heightened consciousness levels allows rulers to be swayed by greed, ambition, ego, and selfishness—a low level of vibrational consciousness that shapes the disorganized and failing societal model we live in.

Those who advocate resolutions through war are nothing but fools lacking a world of faculties. Some may believe they will go unpunished, especially after death—an aspect to be explored later in our discussion. The mysteries of this world are so profound that anyone engaging in wrongdoing and assuming our brief earthly experience will absolve them of accountability is, in essence, a fool. Albert Einstein once remarked, "Two things are infinite, the universe and human stupidity, and I am not yet completely sure about the universe." Can we debate his argument?

The vastness and unknown knowledge hinted at by the sheer size of the universe serve as a colossal signpost, reminding us that our understanding of our purpose and roles in this place, at this point in time, is woefully inadequate. The pursuit of power without first obtaining the knowledge to control it is fallible. A person may feel as powerful as they believe, owing to their position, but their foolishness may blind them until something as minute and invisible as a virus strips away that power—an inescapable blow to our sense of greatness and authority. Such blows leave scars, encouraging humans to reassess their state of consciousness and the true purpose of our existence.

## 13  SCIENCE UNRAVELING THE CREATOR'S GRAND DESIGN

Revisiting the egg theory, let's apply the concept of embryonic development to understand the creation of a fully intelligent and functional human being. Envision a fertilized egg undergoing a series of intricate processes that result in the formation of a highly advanced machine—the human body. Despite our technological advancements, we still grapple with fully comprehending the complexity of the design inherent in our development. The remarkable ability of the human body to undergo self-development unveils a level of sophistication that surpasses our current understanding.

Every physiological function—vision, audition, communication, sensation, movement, olfaction, among others—seems purposefully engineered by our almighty creators. This concept extends beyond human creation to encompass everything that predates us and wasn't constructed by humans. Each natural element serves a distinct purpose—sun, ocean, wind, fire, rocks, plants, and even insects—all contributing to maintaining a delicate balance on our planet and sustaining life within it.

If even the positioning of your fingers, like the strategically placed thumb, has a purpose in enabling you to grasp things perfectly, why would you assume your existence at this precise moment holds no purpose? This notion of applying purpose to our existence may still challenge those dwelling in a low vibrational level of consciousness, but the evolution of our species requires considerable effort and, perhaps, more than one lifetime or a continuing existence in the afterlife. While the idea of multiple existences might spark debate, considering the purposeless existence of a single lifetime contradicts the laws of the universe and renders the entire cosmos devoid of meaning. We will explore this concept further as we move forward.

Addressing the question of who our creator is, technically, it remains unanswered. However, the abundance of evidence suggests a creator exists. To comprehend this, we must refrain from creating numerous versions of a God that diminish its omniscient nature. The perpetual debates about the existence of a God arise from the vast disconnect between the concept and our undeniably limited intelligence.

Throughout human history, the quest for understanding has given rise to countless religions, each attempting to define what a creator is and what it expects from us. Unfortunately, these doctrines, when not approached with caution, have often led to misguided and misconceived notions of right and wrong. In extreme cases, they have even justified acts of terror in the name of the creator. This raises a pivotal question: if the creator is believed to be omnipotent and capable of creating all things according to these doctrines, why would it depend on humans to carry out such extreme actions? Or is this just one of the many absurdities of the human experience?

The human body, on its own, stands as an undeniable masterpiece of work, far beyond our scientific reach—an awe-inspiring testament to the elevated intelligence of our creators. As we grapple with these profound questions, it becomes apparent that the answers lie in the evolution of our species. Exploring the potential within our consciousness could expedite our journey to these answers, but the mystery of our creator persists, challenging us to expand our understanding and move beyond the limitations of our intelligence.

# 14  WEAK LEADERS, BUNKER BUILDERS: THE FEARFUL CONSCIOUS

Bunkers, bunkers, bunkers—the ostentatious display of the super-rich, invested in their own ideals. They believe themselves to be the planet's savviest minds due to their success in building influential companies. However, their illusions of invincibility shatter when a mere virus disrupts the lives of everyone. This prompts a reconsideration of the old saying, "money does not buy happiness"—nor does it ensure good health either. The pandemic has been a harsh lesson, revealing that, perhaps, there are possible hidden agendas at play.

Suddenly, we find ourselves in a reality check, acknowledging the fallibility and vulnerability we conveniently forgot. "Are we truly digging bunkers, or is there more to this?" Take a moment to ponder that; we will come back to it.

Leaders convene at the COP28 UN Climate Change Conference, APEC Summit, and other post-COVID meetings amidst a global economic downturn. Yet, the purpose of these gatherings remains elusive. Post-pandemic, chaos still reigns, fueled by irresponsibility and greed. The question lingers: what were these meetings meant to achieve beyond showcasing a lack of collective foresight to avert global catastrophe?

Since the pandemic, we've initiated wars, battled terrorism, and witnessed the proliferation of ineffective vaccines. In a world where profit overshadows lives, our leaders, incapable of consensus, prioritize their interests over global well-being. While excuses for meetings on climate change happen, world hunger persists. It's the same old story—a select few making decisions for the masses, ensuring their interests prevail. Instead of leveraging their power to build a peaceful world, they seem more intent on constructing bunkers. But for whom? Themselves?

Yes, being a world leader is inherently challenging, but while history applauds leaders like Leonidas, who stood firm for their people with minimal resources, today's leaders can't decide whether to hide underground or flee to outer space. Movies now depict cyberattacks, hinting at an impending end, diverting attention from age-old threats. "Bunkers? Silly me."

Secret bunkers for the super-rich, hidden yet widely known. Celebrities and wealthy figures follow suit, preparing for an apocalypse. This secrecy is as intentional as leaked celebrity scandals. A revealing movie follows. Can we spell "pretext"? Let's halt before treading into risky territory.

We anticipated leaders would offer improved solutions post-pandemic. Alas, we keep colliding without learning life's lessons, driven by the need to assert dominance, feeding insecurities and egos.

Let's explore the misconstrued notions of what power truly entails and how our underdeveloped consciousness shapes these ideas. People have an inherent need to signal their power to others—a gesture that serves to assuage their insecurities and elevate their ego. To illustrate, consider the scenario where an individual drives a Ferrari. Observers, influenced by the sight of this luxury car, may feel a compulsion to own one themselves. However, it begs the question: Was there not a time when Ferraris did not exist? Technically, no one ever needed a Ferrari in the first place. The desire for such possessions stems from a perpetual cycle of comparison, triggering an inferiority mechanism and perpetuating a sense of being left behind in an unending competition.

This pattern of comparison extends beyond possessions such as cars to historical instances where individuals or groups acquired diverse tangible sources to showcase influence or authority. In the era before cars dominated, people engaged in a similar display of status with horses. Whether it was owning a Lipizzaner, an Andalusian, or an Arabian horse, or participating in horse racing with Thoroughbreds—the quest for the superior and more prestigious continued. This mindset persisted through the transition to cars, luxury vehicles, and private jets. The struggle endures, focusing on who possesses the better item and who owns more.

This inclination to constantly compare reflects an underdeveloped subconsciousness, impeding humanity's pace towards evolution. It prompts the question: Do humans genuinely crave equality? In an age where there's a yearning for equal rights, achieving true equality demands overcoming certain faculties like jealousy and greed, fostering a sense of community.

However, the prospect of socialism, as commonly perceived, isn't embraced. The inherent issues of greed and centralized power contradict the principles of equality and freedom within all political systems. Throughout history, political systems have taken various forms, none proving universally beneficial to mankind. The inherent flaw in governance choices often results in desperate constructions—an extent exemplified by building bunkers, an ultimate solution adopted by the super-rich in their endeavor to secure their futures. Regardless of the existence of bunkers, their fate, much like ours, remains mortal. The urgency behind such measures may be a pretext, a recurring theme in history where public promotion hints at a looming threat or a potential cover for a concealed agenda. In the end, the construction of bunkers serves as a tangible manifestation of the uncertainty that the super-rich grapple with as they strive to secure their futures, acknowledging the inevitability of mortality.

# 15  ABORTION AND THE CHICKEN PARADOX

In today's world, our decision-making process is often shaped by a stark, binary approach to politics as views become increasingly polarized. Political propaganda, propelled by the speed of communication, bombards us with opinions from all corners of the globe before we even have a chance to form our own conclusions.

Thanks to social media, we receive instant feedback, and our perspectives are molded by a mix of diverse views, sometimes without us even realizing it. Initially, when we come across a story or a reel on social media, we immediately embrace a formed opinion based on the presented information. However, delving into user comments can quickly reshape our thoughts, pulling us into taking sides rather than allowing us to develop our own nuanced ideas.

Let's explore abortion rights as an example—a topic split between advocates and opponents. I promise to provide an unbiased perspective without taking sides. This involves questioning the false virtues that arise when decisions primarily benefit individuals, overlooking the collective viewpoint of others and all life on this planet.

When it comes to abortion, a complex process that involves the removal of an underdeveloped being from the uterus, opinions range from viewing it as a crime to considering it a choice influenced by survival and Earth's challenges. Rather than prescribing a right or wrong stance, I present various aspects to consider in a holistic manner.

The broader issue may not only involve the decision to proceed with abortion but also how we conduct ourselves in society, often drawing individualistic conclusions based on personal ideals rather than collectively considering the well-being of all humanity. Our quickness to criticize each other for actions that deviate from societal norms becomes evident. Taking the example of global egg consumption, I highlight our tendency to overconsume without moral justification, simply because we can.

To drive this point home, I present a hypothetical scenario involving the return of dinosaurs, framing it as a mirror to our current actions. While seemingly far-fetched, this comparison underscores potential parallels in moral considerations.

Recognizing potential objections regarding the differentiation between abortion, the consumption of unfertilized eggs, or the use of contraceptive pills, it's crucial to emphasize a striking parallel that unveils the hypocrisy ingrained in our decision-making. Imagine for a moment if dinosaurs were present today, possessing greater strength than us. In such a scenario, they might seize our eggs, place them in a pan, and fry them at their whim, simply because they have the power to do so. This mirrors how we, as humans, treat chickens—exerting our strength over them, regardless of their objections.

This comparison vividly illustrates the hypocrisy in human decision-making, particularly concerning abortion. While we engage in a daily practice of aborting chicks, justified by our strength over chickens, we fail to recognize the inconsistency in our ethical stance. This reflection prompts us to reconsider our foundational beliefs and challenges the moral high ground we often assume.

As humans, we stand out as the only species on this planet rapidly contributing to its destruction. In stark contrast, every other animal seems to live in consistent harmony with nature's laws. This prompts a thought: are we truly the rational beings we claim to be, or have our egos overshadowed our capacity for reason? While we often label other animals as irrational due to their differing cognitive capacities, perhaps we should explore their perspectives on us.

Picture this: a lion or a zebra equipped with a mobile phone, spending their day engaging in TikTok dances and sharing their antics with the animal kingdom for likes. It may sound absurd, but this whimsical image serves as a metaphor for our behavior. We, the supposedly advanced beings, resemble underdeveloped creatures with egos so inflated that even an ant can't stand us.

So, when pondering the question of whether abortion is right or wrong in a world where we systematically kill and consume various animals, sometimes even for mere pleasure, does the answer truly matter? Or should we imagine asking dinosaurs how they feel about it, considering they might be the ones putting us in skillets for a delightful eggs Benedict breakfast? This reflection encourages us to reconsider the weight we assign to moral debates in a world where our actions often contradict the harmony observed in the rest of the animal kingdom.

# 16  THE LGBTQ+, HAMAS-ISRAEL ALGORITHMIC SPUR

Over a decade ago, I found myself settling a bet, a whimsical dare orchestrated by my extraordinary friends. Picture this: strolling down the city streets donned in electric blue 70s Saturday Night Fever pants, a daringly pink Freddie Mercury shirt that left my chest proudly exposed, and an exuberant red afro wig crowning my 6'1" tall, dark, and handsome frame. Ready to saunter through the urban jungle, circus circus style, with unabashed confidence.

Oh well, all's fair in jest until I hit the pavement. For a good ten minutes, I waded through a sea of relentless teasing, laughter echoing through the air, and even some unsolicited harassment. Until, that is, three figures emerged from the crowd, eyes ablaze with a threatening intensity, demanding I move aside. In a heartbeat, I shed the flamboyant wig and, in my resonant, Denzel Washington-esque voice, I posed a simple question, "Yo, my dudes, we got a problem?"

It was as if they'd stumbled onto the set of a blockbuster movie – the tough bravado they'd assumed melted away, replaced by a sudden softness. Instead of succumbing to the bubbling rage within me, urging me to give them a lesson they wouldn't forget, I paused. I entertained a thought, observing how humans often display toughness when they perceive an advantage. I chose not to impose on them what they had intended to impose on me. So, I bared my soul. I articulated that this daring escapade was nothing but a playful dare, leading to an unexpected encounter with the realities others endure.

As I navigated the world through the lens of the costume I wore, I realized I was stepping into the shoes of those confronting prejudice – whether it be the LGBTQ+ community, different races, religions, body types, or genders. In that transformative moment, I unveiled a profound truth: our biases, racism, and prejudices all originate from the same source – the minds of individuals vibrating at a lower frequency, overshadowed by the veil of ignorance.

I have always rejected prejudice against individuals, embracing a stance against evil. I believe that standing united against malevolence, rather than turning against each other, is the key to preventing its reign in our lives.

Now, let's delve into a controversial issue within the LGBTQ+ communities concerning gender identity matters, especially in the context of children's rights. The genesis of this issue lies in a peculiar trend that emerged. It started with an individual making an unconventional self-identification through a video and social media post – "I identify as letmegetcreativesexual." While intended to illustrate a point, it sparked widespread criticism due to its seeming oddity. The situation escalated as social media algorithms capitalized on the trend, causing it to go viral. Corporations, including TV networks, joined the bandwagon to exploit this trend for financial gain. The government, equipped with greater powers, followed suit, going a step further by enacting legislations and laws to support it, all in pursuit of retaining votes and/or securing their interests. This phenomenon, driven by profit motives, spiraled out of control. The genuine interests of various communities, whether LGBTQ+, racial, or ethnic, got lost in the exploitation. Even members within these communities grew disenchanted with the situation.

This exploitation isn't exclusive to matters of identity; it extends to global events. Much like the handling of the Hamas attack on Israel, where media, TV networks, and the government leverage the situation for financial gains. Propaganda on Palestinians and Israelis becomes a tool for profit, with little regard for the chaos it inflicts on people.

In essence, the issue lies not in the diverse identities or global events themselves, but in the exploitation driven by financial motives. It's crucial to discern the genuine concerns of communities from the profit-driven narratives perpetuated by various entities.

A call to action emerges – if we truly desire peace and acceptance, we must exhibit respect and love toward all humanity. Let's unite against evil rather than turning against each other. Ceasing these over-and-over discussions is key to preventing governments and businesses from profiting from these matters. With a powerful reminder that speaking from the heart and embracing unity is the path to true change, ensuring that we are not just seeking personal benefits but contributing to a world where love triumphs over prejudice.

# 17  VIRTUAL REALITIES: SOCIAL MEDIA AND THE DISTORTIONS OF REALITY

In the profound exploration of modern relationships, this topic emerges as one of the most challenging to discuss, primarily due to the adept distortion of relationship realities by contemporary society. It is imperative to begin this discourse by dispelling the notion that individuals claiming happiness in solitude are merely deceiving themselves. Despite encountering a series of failed relationships, it is crucial to acknowledge that the absence of a loved one does not negate the human necessity for companionship. The innate craving for love is deeply ingrained within us, whether we choose to acknowledge it or not. It's a built-in mechanism required for procreation. In modern society, individuals claim that they do not need anyone in their lives, and that they are fully happy on their own. The fallibility of our society to distort the ideals of companionship does not equate to the lack of our needs to pursue the same.

Earlier discussions have alluded to the imperative need for self-discovery and an understanding of our limitations. This underscores the notion that one cannot expect to bring happiness to others without first ensuring contentment within oneself. The pursuit of co-dependency is debunked as an illusory path to a happy life. Oftentimes, individuals enter relationships burdened with heavy emotional baggage, mistakenly believing that such connections will alleviate their burdens. However, a plate becomes prone to spilling when additional weight is added to an already overloaded plate.

A critical issue lies in the very selection of partners. A single day spent with a new acquaintance can foster the illusion of having found "the one" – a home run to everlasting happiness. Yet, the naivety of such assumptions becomes evident over time. These considerations predominantly pertain to the individual, aspects that necessitate examination long before embarking on a journey with someone barely known. Unfortunately, reality diverges from this ideal scenario, as individuals often rely on their imagination to create a version of their prospective partner—a version confined to the realms of fantasy.

Consider the whimsical scenario of envisioning a romantic brunch in Paris, set against the backdrop of a luxurious hotel or a castle courtyard surrounded by nature's splendor. Such cinematic aspirations, crafted as directors of our own nonsensical ideas, often lead to disappointment when, after two years in a relationship, the anticipated trip to Paris remains unrealized.

This tendency to craft unrealistic expectations is not a solitary act. It becomes increasingly precarious when both individuals involved engage in this practice. What ensues is a combustible mixture, a passcode combination activating a ticking bomb. Many perpetuate this cycle, reaching mistaken conclusions that solitude is synonymous with happiness, inadvertently mummifying love and imposing a lifetime ban on its acknowledgment.

The exploration extends into the domain of social media, a space where distorted portrayals of relationships frequently command attention. Within this virtual landscape, the depiction of disillusioned versions contributes to a narrative suggesting that relationships are not worth pursuing. This narrative fosters the belief that people are more inclined toward transient adventures lacking commitment. Here, individuals of genuine goodwill find themselves wounded by the actions of those less virtuous, who, in a cruel twist, often undergo a transformation, becoming versions of the less virtuous themselves. This unsettling cycle perpetuates a disheartening evolution, where the virtuous may, over time, succumb to the very behaviors that once caused them harm, adding to the complexity of the emotional terrain in the realm of love.

Seeking solace in advice from close friends, who themselves bear the scars of untreated wounds from failed relationships, exacerbates the situation. This pattern resembles a pandemic, a virus eradicating love from a world infected by its own distorted perceptions. The prevailing question echoes: "Are there any good ones left on this planet?" The unequivocal answer resounds—an affirmative "yes." A world teeming with remarkable individuals awaits, but the key to discovering such a match lies in dismantling the nonsensical blocks constructed in our minds, the idealized image reminiscent of perfection found in Disney fairy tales.

To embark on this journey successfully, one must cultivate acts of generosity, charity, and benevolence toward others. It entails dedicating time to explore companionship, friendship, understanding, and, eventually, love. Without mastering the art of self-sacrifice and wholeheartedly giving to one's significant other, love remains incomplete. The poignant term "My Better Half" underscores the necessity for mutual selflessness. Any relationship devoid of this balance, characterized by a lopsided distribution of love, is akin to a battleground where selfishness clashes with selflessness, ultimately leading to catastrophic consequences.

In the pursuit for love, the fundamental principle persists: love should unfold as a mutual, rhythmic exchange, a seamless dance transcending arbitrary percentages. The essence is not to measure affection with an 80% contribution from one party and a meager 20% from the other. Recognizing this imbalance and heeding the warning signs, one is implored to step out immediately, awaiting a partner willing to meet halfway. In unraveling the complexities of modern relationships, the key lies not in solitude or disillusionment but in dismantling misconceptions and embracing the genuine, reciprocal, and complete nature of love.

In the complexities of forging connections, one often disregards the subtle cues, the telltale signs of red flags encountered when meeting someone new. Amid the exhilaration of this initial encounter, physical attraction frequently eclipses deeper considerations.

Red flags, however, serve as purposeful guides and should not be dismissed lightly. They do not necessarily brand someone as inherently "bad" or "evil," but rather signal that this individual might not align harmoniously with your own values. Dismissing these signals with the clichéd notion that "opposites attract" can be faulty. Picture attempting to unite a basketball player, reveling in the indulgences of bars and nightclubs, with a person who relishes quiet evenings reading books and listening to classical music. Despite the allure of opposites, such divergent lifestyles may pave the way for long-term catastrophe.

Establishing foundational principles early in a relationship is crucial, not to confine the other person but to define mutual boundaries that foster understanding. For those advocating a free-spirited existence and open relationships, the authenticity of motives becomes paramount. It is vital to ascertain that such choices stem from genuine openness rather than serving as a façade for underlying selfish motivations. Clarity and open communication, from the outset, lay the groundwork for a relationship with a higher chance of enduring success.

# 18 THE NETFLIX PARADOX OF LOVE: THE ILLUSION OF ENDLESS CHOICES

Allow me to introduce you to the Netflix theory of relationships, an analogy that illustrates the challenges modern love faces. Picture this: you turn on the TV, launch Netflix, and start browsing for a movie. Most of the time, you find yourself endlessly scrolling without choosing the perfect film. The vast array of options overwhelms your decision-making process. Remember the days of manually flipping channels when TV choices were limited? You would pick a channel and stick with it for the day.

Today, in our app-driven world of romantic connections, seeking the right partner mirrors the Netflix movie search. Opening an app like Tinder, you spend hours swiping left or right, matching with numerous potential partners. The abundance of choices makes it challenging to decide on the perfect match. However, this contemporary method of finding a partner introduces its own set of challenges.

Modern relationships often face the hurdle of longevity. The perception of having a multitude of other options creates a mindset where individuals may quickly judge and abandon a relationship at the first sign of imperfection. Similar to stopping a movie after 10 minutes because you recall there are more interesting options. This cycle perpetuates, leaving individuals entangled in a web of choices, none meeting the ideal perfection they seek.

Yet, perfection is an unattainable standard for any human partner; a successful relationship requires overcoming challenges together, evolving as a couple, and learning from one another to achieve the desired level of development.

In the past, people physically walked to meet others, limiting interactions to local spaces such as schools or workplaces. One had to physically travel to meet someone, unsure of what to expect upon arrival. There was no preview of cultural aesthetics or background; everything had to be discovered in real-time.

Engaging in relationships demanded effort, as one had to walk out of the house and actively participate in a series of encounters. This investment made it less likely for individuals to easily abandon relationships. Similarly, in the old days when you had to walk out of your house to rent a movie at Blockbuster, the options were there, but you would choose carefully. The effort it took to find one, added to the risk of picking the wrong one, outweighed the worthiness of even taking such a trip.

The struggle to maintain relationships today can be attributed, in part, to the minimal effort required in the digital age. Technological progress now enables connections from anywhere globally, transforming the traditional approach to relationship building. You can be in New York, getting to know someone in Dubai, or in Rome, establishing connections with individuals in Rio de Janeiro. The geographical barriers that once confined relationships to local spaces have been dismantled.

Apps provide a preview of interactions, allowing individuals to formulate well-thought-out questions and answers. This premeditation permits the creation of a persona that may not necessarily reflect the true self. Contrastingly, in the past, all interactions happened in real-time, fostering genuine connections. Some argue that a drawback in the past was that individuals often remained in relationships even if they were not truly happy. While there is truth in this perspective, there is also the aspect where people exerted considerable effort to sustain relationships, only to eventually part ways.

In contemporary society, the tendency is for individuals to invest minimal effort in relationships, a trend that significantly contributes to the elevated rates of separation and divorce.

This challenge is part of a more extensive issue. People are influenced by the desire to present an idealized version of their lives, fueled by the pressures of social media. The pursuit of this "perfect" life can lead to anxiety, frustration, and financial strain, impacting relationships negatively. The pervasive use of apps encourages the portrayal of a reality detached from actual experiences.

Considering the earlier example in the reading of a dreamt trip to Paris, individuals may struggle in their relationships not because they want or need to go to Paris, but because they have already imagined the couple's photo with the Eiffel Tower in the background. This desire for a fantasy can often go beyond travel alone, extending to other luxurious ideas, such as expensive weddings that result in anxiety, frustrations, financial losses, and at times, become at the cost of their relationships.

A single day of extravagance for the sake of portraying an unrealistic achievement can lead to lasting consequences. This pursuit, often driven by social media validation, may bring momentary satisfaction but can lead to financial strain and distress. In essence, the quest for an illusionary ideal, often fueled by addictive app usage, becomes a significant hurdle in modern relationships.

53

# 19  PAIN IN MEDICAL FAILURES: A MARTIAN MEDICINE

Before unveiling into my insights on the vibrational effects that contribute to depression, suicide, and other diseases within the context of these pages, it's crucial to emphasize that this content does not serve as a replacement for medical or psychological advice. Instead, its purpose is to explore spiritual perspectives and reveal how eliminating specific negative energies from our daily lives can act as a protective shield against the unforeseen challenges woven into the fabric of our existence.

Imagine a life that seems normal, where things follow a reasonable rhythm. However, challenges are bound to arise at some point, perhaps multiple times over a lifetime. These challenges, often accompanied by the heaviness of sadness and stress, are energies that seem to appear without warning. Consider, for instance, the deep pain of an unexpected abandonment, like a spouse leaving without notice or explanation. In many cases, lower vibrational energies flood a person's emotions faster than they can cope. It's as though life propels an asteroid at an alarming speed, and upon impact, everything comes to a halt.

For a moment, let's venture into the fantastical realm of "The Martian," a cinematic journey featuring Matt Damon and birthed from the pen of Andy Weir. This narrative captures the lone struggle of an astronaut surviving on Mars after a tumultuous dust storm compels the crew spacecraft to take off, leaving him stranded. Without immersing ourselves in the intricate plot and mindful of those yet to witness this cinematic marvel, there's a pivotal moment where the astronaut is queried about his survival on Mars. Channeling the spirit of Mark Watney, played by Matt Damon, his response encapsulates the essence of resilience, transcending the confines of fiction. "You just begin. You do the math. You solve one problem... and you solve the next one... and then the next. And if you solve enough problems, you get to come home." This declaration underscores the profound lesson for us humans in our ephemeral sojourn—to embark on the laborious task of addressing life's challenges. Regardless of their intensity, we must endeavor to resolve problem after problem until the sanctuary of home is regained.

Returning to the scenario of sudden abandonment by a spouse, finding yourself alone prompts a process of self-reflection. You replay a myriad of situations in your head, blaming yourself at one point and then experiencing rage towards your spouse the next. What's happening mirrors the isolation of being left alone on Mars. If you succumb to sadness, cry, become depressed, and contemplate death in your head every day, you will eventually yield to the circumstances that caught you off guard. So, what do you do at this point? Do you succumb to despair, or do you embark on solving problem after problem to ensure your safety? It entails holding your head up high, engaging in the necessary work, and enduring the painful journey until you arrive safely back home—restoring the joyous essence of your existence.

In a certain phase of my life, I developed an autoimmune disorder that shifted my existence from a healthy and happy state into a swimming pool filled with a river of symptoms. This journey spanned 51 doctors and over 260 visits to various specialized practitioners over five years. I felt like I had left this Earth through a comma, facing incredibly difficult challenges that never seemed to restore me to my normal self. Sadness, stress and pain, accompanied by a mix of other emotions, settled in. At times, doctors even thought it was all in my head. Some suggested beach visits for relaxation, while others scheduled treatments for mainstream diseases. Amidst a cacophony of symptoms, each diagnosis revealed nothing abnormal—clean blood tests, optimal nutrient levels. I, a seemingly healthy individual, found myself ensnared in a labyrinth of unexplained suffering.

Did I contemplate giving up during those five long years? Undoubtedly so. After a mere three months into this tumultuous odyssey, the weight of despair felt sufficiently burdensome to entertain the notion of exchanging it for all the wealth the world could offer. Although the belief that money can buy everything, the elusive nature of happiness and health persists. So I turned around, thinking that maybe I was trying to solve this in the wrong way. On one of my worst days, I did something quite unconventional—I hugged a tree, contemplating that perhaps the solution lay in a different direction. I know what you may be thinking: "He must have lost it." This unconventional act signified my decision to halt seeking help from doctors. Recognizing the medical industry as nothing more than a financial instrument, I sought help from the only place that made more sense—the natural world.

The lingering question may arise—did it work? Indeed, it did. However, the journey was far from the conventional narrative of incessant prayers eradicating all tribulations. Instead, my approach involved a deliberate decision to immerse myself fully in a situation resembling the challenges depicted in the Martian predicament. The goal was not to avoid but to confront and overcome these challenges using alternative means. The initial step involved cultivating immunity against defeat, purging every negative thought. This included blocking out sadness, depression, anxiety, and other low-level vibrational energies that were flooding into my head, barricading any room for courage, hope, faith, and other emotions that could aid in building mental strength. Each morning, I strolled by the tree and engaged in a conversation, playfully dubbing it Greenie. "Good morning, Greenie, I'm on my way. Wish me luck," became a daily ritual. The challenge was that pain consistently sent signals to my brain, conflicting with thoughts essential for my well-being. Determined, I chose to ignore these conflicting signals. A memory surfaced, recalling a scene from YouTube featuring Trautman, a snippet from the movie Rambo, where he asserted, "I'm telling you that Rambo is a machine. A man who's trained to ignore pain..." Channeling that resolve, I adopted the persona of Matt Stallone—a soldier from outer space steadfastly ignoring pain while navigating the challenging terrain of Mars. Swiftly, the landscape of my experiences began to transform. In my quest to surmount obstacles, I delved into extensive research, seeking a profound understanding of the intricacies of our bodies, the dynamics of pain, and drawing insights from scientific studies. A fortuitous encounter with a physiotherapist from another land blossomed into friendship. Discussions on the potency of positive thinking as a beacon of light even in the darkest of life's stages became a common refrain. An innocuous coffee outing with this newfound confidante led to a pivotal question— "Would you care for some sugar in your coffee?" It sparked a revelation—an intricate web connecting sugar to adrenal glands, pancreas, diabetes, cancer, metabolism, fat retention, and stomach lining. A stringent diet already in place, the elimination of sugar for two weeks showcased discernible changes by Day 3.

As improvement materialized, the fortification of confidence and the cultivation of positive thinking gathered momentum within. Low vibrational energies dissipated, fatigue waned, muscles surged with strength, and the pall of pain began to lift. Running became plausible, breathing resumed its natural rhythm, anxiety abated, and engagement in sports and workouts unfolded seamlessly. Each passing day felt like a return home, culminating in an experience that imparted profound wisdom. Since this transformative juncture, I've mastered the art of blocking these low vibrational energies, cultivating a life adorned with joy. Almost effortlessly, life's offerings flow in a natural rhythm, fostering a profound sense of contentment. A wish emerged—this wisdom had graced my early years. Yet, perhaps the essence of our journey lies in the perpetual evolution through these challenges that transformed me into a vastly different individual. I am now profoundly attuned to the intricacies of life, and through it, I've gained an understanding of life, death, and the intentions behind the cosmos.

# 20 THE KAIOWAS TRIBE: LAST STAND AGAINST MEN

In the confines of my room, I found myself, just a kid strumming my acoustic guitar alongside my percussionist buddy. Amid our musical pursuits, my mother, the embodiment of drama, shouted at us to lower our jam, all because she yearned to watch her soap opera. "Brazilians love soap operas, don't they?" I chuckled to myself, knowing that my mom's dramatic flair could rival any Oscar-winning performance.

Nevertheless, we persisted in our musical endeavors, playing the song "Kaiowas" by a band called Sepultura. In the midst of our musical transcendence, I abruptly halted, interrupting my buddy with the query, "What is Kaiowas, anyway?" Instruments dropped, and we left. Yes, indeed, we ventured straight to the library. "What? You went to a Library?" you might ask. Indeed, kind sir, Uncle Google was not around to enlighten us with information whenever our hearts desired. Our news, unlike the lightning speed of modern updates, traversed at the pace of a leisurely walk – and by that, I mean a lot of walking.

Now, brace yourself for this revelation – we discovered that the Kaiowá, also known as Guarani-Kaiowá, are indigenous people residing in three South American countries: Paraguay, the Brazilian state of Mato Grosso do Sul, and northeastern Argentina. Their lands remained relatively undisturbed until the 1800s when settlers began encroaching upon them. These tribes faced gradual displacement due to deforestation driven by the profitability of settler's agro-businesses.

As children, that wasn't quite the revelation we anticipated. I recall our discussions lasting for hours each time we jammed to that song, concluding with a profound sense of respect.

As our initial readings faded from memory, what remained was the haunting knowledge that the tribes were committing mass suicides in response to the government's invasion of their lands. The upcoming discussion will delve deeper into these tragic events, shedding light on the historical and cultural contexts that led to such drastic measures. In the concluding chapters, I will emphasize the importance of incorporating this critical topic into our book, illustrating its significance in fostering awareness and understanding of the challenges faced by indigenous communities.

In October 2012, a group of 170 Kaiowás, encamped for nearly a year near a river in Mato Grosso do Sul, Brazil, declared their readiness to accept extinction following an eviction order from a federal judge. Their letter stated,

*"...we know that we are going, and we want to be killed and buried with our ancestors here where we are today, so we ask the Government and the Federal Justice not to decree our eviction/expulsion, but we request to decree our collective death and to bury us everybody here. We ask, once and for all, to decree our decimation and total extinction, in addition to sending several tractors to dig a large hole to throw and bury*

*our bodies."*

This heart-wrenching plea was part of a letter from the Guarani-Kaiowá of Pyelito Kue in 2012.

A decade prior, back in that time, minimal progress had been made in demarcating indigenous territories in Brazil, notably for the Guarani-Kaiowá people. During that period, violence against indigenous communities in the state escalated, marked by leader assassinations and frequent attacks by gunmen. Various Guarani-Kaiowá communities, including Potrero Guasu, Arroio Korá, and Laranjeira Nhanderu, were subjected to intensified aggression in the preceding weeks.

In response to these attacks, social movements staged a demonstration in Brasília to defend the Guarani-Kaiowá, symbolized by the planting of five thousand crosses on the Esplanada dos Ministérios, the Esplanade of Ministries, highlighting what protesters labeled as "genocide." A petition titled "Prevent the Collective Suicide of the Guarani-Kaiowá Indians" amassed 21,000 signatures on the Avaaz platform, reflecting the grim reality that the Guarani-Kaiowá faced one of the highest suicide rates in the country and globally. Ministry of Health data revealed that every six days, a young Guarani-Kaiowá took their own life, with 555 suicides reported from 2000 onwards, predominantly by hanging (98%) and committed by men (70%), mostly aged 15 to 29. The alarming rates of suicide and homicide were attributed to insufficient land, a lack of demarcated territories, and confinement in indigenous reserves. Reports from Cimi indicated that Mato Grosso do Sul had become the leading state in indigenous homicides, with the Guarani-Kaiowá described as a people facing cultural and political assassination, whether due to government indifference or hired gunmen acting on behalf of landowners.

Consider this: everything you've encountered in this book so far, leading up to this moment, appears almost otherworldly in its detachment from the human race. The cruelty, ego, and greed exhibited by humans are but manifestations of lower-level vibrational individuals, easily propelled into committing acts such as the mass extinction of peaceful communities, all to satisfy settlers' profit motives.

I vividly remember my friend expressing a desire to leave this planet. I responded with a jest, "Sorry, buddy, you can't. God made it round for a reason, fortified with tons of gravitational forces to ensure us egomaniacs and sinners won't venture far without the Creator's consent." "Ain't that something?" he laughed. We'll delve deeper into gravitational forces later.

I won't expand into an Indigenous history lesson, as most are already aware of their tragic plight. However, I can unequivocally state that they exemplify living in harmony with nature, God, and the universe. They thrive without a fraction of the clutter we've constructed for our survival. Picture approaching a Native and inquiring about their interest in health insurance. Their likely response: "Can't we continue receiving healing from the ground?" Persist in pushing your sales tactics, and you might stress the poor Native to the point of dropping dead right in front of you. Congratulations, you've just claimed your first Native customer fatality.

Observe how Natives collaboratively support one another for the greater good, in stark contrast to our world where individualistic gains prevail. This contrast is a breeding ground for immense suffering. Chimps, dolphins, wolves, and Natives exhibit collective efforts, especially during hunting, while humans indulge in the fast-food mantra – "I want my food, and I want it fast, please."

Scholars estimate that 50 to 100 million Natives inhabited the Americas before European contact, losing up to 90% of their population—the eradication of exemplars of the species we should aspire to become. Some argue that seizing opportunities is intrinsic to human nature, drawing parallels with animal behavior. Indeed, animals, akin to Natives, kill for survival, adhering to nature's laws. They comply with Nature's law, acting upon necessities and controlling our natural habitats, as Nature alone will eventually enforce such.

However, some may argue that the earlier Dinosaur discussion in the book was meant to indicate that the strongest call all the shots. Instead, it aimed to illustrate the potential consequences if they behaved at the same distorted level of consciousness as we humans do. Most animals, as demonstrated by Natives, live in perfect harmony with the natural laws of this planet. In contrast, we humans engage in killings out of greed, entertainment, anger, and many other incoherent acts, driven by ignorance and deprived wisdom.

During the COVID-19 pandemic, as lockdowns and restrictions confined humans, urban areas experienced a significant decline in human presence and activity. This led to an extraordinary phenomenon: a surge in animal sightings in urban environments. With reduced human disturbance and fewer people on the streets, animals that typically avoid human activity felt safer to explore these areas.

Regardless of our agreement, this presented an opportunity to reveal humanity's perception among all other creatures on the planet. Animals were perhaps rejoicing and thinking, "Are they gone for good? Let's celebrate." Wild goats, pumas, coyotes, sea turtles, marine mammals, and birds were observed in the urban areas and coastal regions due to the absence of humans. This phenomenon served as Nature's voice, urging us to shift our focus for elevation. Failure to do so may subject us to prolonged stages of suffering, a consequence of our own actions. However, we have the power to avoid such pain by addressing and rectifying our misguided behaviors.

Regrettably, the transformation required to eliminate these lower vibrational levels of consciousness spans beyond the scope of a single lifetime, a concept we'll explore further later on. For now, understand that history serves as a testament, capturing the subtle but definitive changes that highlight our evolution. Consider the span of 40,000 to 400,000 years ago, during the era of Neanderthals. Picture their limited knowledge compared to the sophistication of Julius Caesar's time, the Late Republic, and the establishment of the Roman Empire. The pace of human evolution, though gradual, has brought us to a point where life today is a paradise compared to epochs past.

While the struggles of contemporary existence persist, envision a future where lower levels of consciousness—hate, anger, ego, greed— gradually dissipate from our planet. As these negativities vanish, we not only approach a genuine paradise but also unlock the inherent powers and intelligence anticipated by our creators.

# 21  RETIREMENT, AND UNFULFILLED DREAMS

Let's embark on another journey in that DeLorean, soaring into the uncharted territories of the Future. A place I have yet to explore, but my curiosity propels me forward. Imagine reaching the age of 68, having meticulously completed the necessary steps for retirement. Here I stand, on the threshold of a new chapter. Congratulations to me! I am now as old as mountains, figuratively speaking, since I am not really 68 at the time this was written. But back to the Future, weathered by time and ready to emulate the steadfast presence of those ancient peaks. Yet, with this age comes a shift; the ability to walk, run, and revel in festivities diminishes. Isn't it intriguing? A lifetime of hard work and contributions to society, only to retire at an age that limits the enjoyment of the fruits of labor.

And who crafted these rules? The very architects of societal frameworks, orchestrating governance while often leading lives detached from the constraints imposed on the masses. It unfolds as a paradox—a dedication to societal progression leading to retirement at an age that restricts the ability to fully relish the rewards. The whims of rule-makers reverberate through the lives of ordinary citizens.

Now, let's explore the diverse perspectives that color our world. Each individual sees it through a unique lens—some find beauty, others discern shadows and darkness. The world becomes a place of repose, amusement, conquest, or myriad other interpretations.

Consider the notion of conquest, where force is employed to bend others to one's will. Picture being a leader or governor, entrusted with the authority to shape rules aligning with personal ideas and needs. Would one allow policies conflicting with self-interest? Unlikely. Leaders and governors, much like anyone else, design rules according to their visions.

Every law, whether in the United States or elsewhere, likely stems from leaders who seek to mold the world according to their preferences. In a sense, democracy is a mechanism to prevent people from feeling like total slaves, offering basic living conditions through policies that control and prevent sudden overturns of power. The leaders recognize that the current population, having swelled over centuries, could potentially challenge their authority. They understand that suppressing the people could lead to a bloodshed they fear the most—stripping them of everything they possess.

Without advocating for upheaval, let's shed light on the choices we make during our time on Earth. Rarely do we actively advocate for the rights we inherently deserve, allowing leaders to strip them away through ongoing exploitation fueled by fear, lack of wisdom, and an absence of collective consciousness.

This extends beyond governance to the workplace, where exploitation often thrives. Many organizations are moving away from this mindset to prevent management from engaging in exploitative practices. Yet, such events persist today. What if we lived in a world devoid of fear? What if those who believe they wield absolute power haven't disclosed that they fear just as much as the rest? Fear of tomorrow, fear of other leaders, fear of an imaginary enemy seizing their perceived power. Those who believe they control the world are unwittingly playing themselves as fools.

Inside every individual resides a world of fears that governs who we are and how we navigate this brief journey on Earth. Note the constant competition in the workplace—each person vying for a promotion, driven by fear. Most toil in jobs they dislike, overworking for promotions instead of building something enjoyable. Even when the coveted promotion finally arrives, it often fails to deliver the gratification anticipated.

Imagine living a lifetime making choices that yield the least happiness or freedom.

As you navigate through the wisdom within these pages, I invite you to pause—take a moment to deeply reflect on the course your life has charted thus far. In the current landscape, the DeLorean remains a figment of imagination, unable to whisk you backward or propel you forward through time. Liberate yourself from the clutches of fears that may be hindering your journey; expel them from the very fabric of your consciousness.

Release the relentless grip of time from your aspirations, as its presence often begets anxiety and needless concerns. Opt to work not merely arduously, but with the purpose of relishing each moment. Working diligently without mastering the art of maintaining a serene state of consciousness can only lead to suffering—the very adversary you aim to sidestep. In the unfolding chapters of self-discovery, you'll come to realize that your achievements need not carry the weighty burdens we frequently shoulder. We, as creators, shape our own path.

## 22  WHEN THE WIND CHALLENGES GRAVITATIONAL POLICIES

Without getting too deeply into scientific intricacies, have you ever pondered the existence of gravity? All living beings on Earth are somehow anchored at a specific level around the globe. Venture too deep towards the core, and pressure builds against your body. Head towards outer space, and you'll experience conditions akin to higher altitudes, potentially leading to hypoxia and other challenges. This equilibrium keeps all life on Earth within a specific territory, prompting the question: where does this cosmic equilibrium originate?

Consider the wind – on a global scale, the average wind speed at Earth's surface is approximately 3 to 4 meters per second (m/s) or 11 to 14 kilometers per hour (km/h), with some variability across regions. But who ensures that winds adhere to these norms? Without such regulation, walking down the street might expose us to winds of unpredictable speeds. For instance, a sudden gust at 400 meters per second, a force that could be lethal. Fortunately, Earth's environment is regulated, allowing for our continued existence.

Imagine an unregulated Earth where Category 5 winds (157 mph or higher) occur regularly – life as we know it might be eradicated. Now, consider ocean levels. We cherish the sun at the beach, blissfully unaware that nature's regulations prevent ocean levels from rising to heights that could endanger humanity. The Sun and Earth's core adhere to policies to maintain their temperatures, preventing catastrophic extremes. What if rain ceased or our soil stopped yielding crops? Fish are confined to the ocean depths, lacking the ability to traverse the skies, while birds, capable of soaring through the air, find themselves unable to navigate underwater. Our world is purposefully structured with elements that enable the continuation of our existence, but the question lingers – who placed them there and why? Why do these regulations exist, allowing us to participate in life only under specific conditions and in controlled environments?

Despite these evident regulations, there are individuals who still doubt the existence of a higher power, a creator, or a God responsible for everything on our planet. These clear demonstrations occur regularly, yet our minds, perhaps less adept than mollusks in comprehending the vastness of the universe's knowledge, persist in ignoring them. We often form conclusions based on our egocentric and egoistic viewpoints, dismissing the ample evidence surrounding us.

Consider the analogy of our bodies as avatars. Do we not, at times, feel as though we inhabit a borrowed, highly advanced bot that allows us to remotely control a genetically engineered body to play a role? Could it be that we are naive to dismiss the existence of something more powerful than us, especially after witnessing nature's subtle demonstrations? Einstein, in his many arguments, acknowledged the potential for human shortcomings, pointing to the idea that the universe is vast and incomprehensible, while human actions and behaviors can sometimes seem less rational. We will explore why I reference Einstein for the second time in this book and further highlight the power inherent in science, emphasizing its crucial role in the evolution of our species.

I believe we have a long way to go before attaining the comprehension we need, particularly when the concerns of our world often resemble those of a child. Building apps like TikTok and Instagram, the entire planet indulges in sharing childish content. No offense to the creators; their crafts were well-intended. However, our current state of evolution limits us to underdeveloped pursuits.

In summary, connecting this section to gravitational forces aims to emphasize the integral relationship between our endeavors to explore beyond Earth and the acquisition of knowledge. Our pursuit to venture into other cosmic realms, seeking insights into our true essence on Earth, advances in tandem with the pace of knowledge acquisition. Redirecting our focus from perpetual indulgence in entertainment and leisure towards a dedicated pursuit of knowledge has the potential to hasten our exploration of other cosmic landscapes. This shift in focus not only accelerates our cosmic exploration but also holds the promise of unveiling a profound understanding of our existence on Earth.

# 23 ARE WE NOT OF THIS EARTH? UNVEILING OUR EXTRATERRESTRIAL IDENTITY

At this juncture in our scientific understanding, consensus points to compelling evidence that the presence of particles in a protoplanetary disk is intrinsic to the formation of planets throughout the cosmos. By this rationale, it follows that human beings, along with all manifestations of life on Earth today, have extraterrestrial origins. Despite residing on Earth in our current time, we are, in essence, products of outer space—a concept often overlooked or neglected in our educational systems.

Stay with me; clarity will eventually come to sight. Now, armed with the knowledge that we are, in fact, extraterrestrial beings, we can bring clarity to the ambiguities surrounding our existence. This realization challenges oversimplified ideologies about the true sources of our nature. In essence, we are residues of particles and various forms that originated from outer space, other celestial bodies, and possibly even older planets.

Consider Earth's formation approximately 4.6 billion years ago, as suggested by scientific understanding. If we could encapsulate and assimilate all the knowledge amassed over this immense span, we would essentially possess an intelligence akin to that of a godly entity when compared to individuals currently present on Earth.

Let's imagine, for a moment, that humans have an average lifespan of 100 years. This duration equates to a mere 0.0000021739% of the 4.6 billion years. Technically, this represents the percentage of time allotted for an individual to accumulate knowledge during one lifetime compared to the age of Earth itself. In other words, our accumulated knowledge in one lifetime is a spectacle when compared to the existence of Earth alone.

Factual scientific historical evidence, based on detailed records and precise dating methods, extends back only a few thousand years from today. This means we can observe and confirm events that have been documented. While theoretical approaches have significantly contributed to our understanding, estimating Earth's age at around 4.6 billion years, even if we were to live for thousands of years in one lifetime, it would represent just 0.00004348% of the total knowledge since Earth's inception. Although both factual evidence and theoretical concepts complement each other, over an extended period equivalent to thousands of years, it would still be insufficient for a human to amass a comprehensive understanding of life in a single lifetime alone.

Acknowledging the practical challenges of this approach without delving into complex mathematical discussions, the key takeaway is that our knowledge is insufficient to comprehend even a minute fraction of Earth's history, let alone the entire universe. By this definition, we remain relatively primitive beings in the grand scope of the universe, notwithstanding our educational attainments or accumulated wealth.

Still in the cosmic comparisons, despite our advancements, we struggle to devise swift means of transportation to the moon, which is relatively close. If we were to inquire whether the universe is infinite, our responses may vary; yet, a subconscious uncertainty often lingers, grappling with the inconceivable notion of an endless cosmos.

Similarly, our perception of time is tethered to beginnings and endings, likely influenced by the familiar cycles of birth and death. As we contemplate the past, present, and future, the possibility may exist that only memories, present moments, and imagination constitute the true components, collapsing into the present alone. This underscores the importance of being present in our lives on Earth.

Emphasizing the significance of living in the present allows us to connect with experiences in the moment and shields us from accumulating energies detrimental to our evolution. In conclusion, living on Earth becomes more meaningful when we recognize that our existence may equate to a minuscule fraction of time, or potentially even less. Freed from unnecessary worries, fears, and anxieties about death, we can embrace a straightforward and happier existence— being born, experiencing life, and moving forward after death. This opens up the possibility of an eternal or as vast as the laws of the universe allow existence.

In conclusion, our knowledge, when compared to the vastness of the universe, is but a minuscule particle in its cosmic expanse. Therefore, it becomes paramount to live life fully in the present moment, unburdened by unnecessary worries and concerns. Even the fear of or life after death, though not explicitly acknowledged by many religious doctrines, can be set aside. While religious beliefs may differ, each asserting its unique perspective, there is a common thread—they all emphasize the importance of salvation for an afterlife. However, embracing the present moment with a sense of liberation from earthly apprehensions allows us to navigate life more joyfully, appreciating the fleeting nature of our existence on this cosmic stage.

# 24  THE ROOTS OF PREJUDICE UNMASKED

Picture yourself as a deity, the creator of Earth. You sculpt this planet meticulously and breathe life into tiny beings, granting them the profound gift of free will. You shape the world round, a cosmic boundary to contain the unfolding drama. As you watch from your divine vantage point, the spectacle of human behavior unfolds.

In one corner of your creation, groups vie for dominance, invading territories with the fervor of conquest. In another, a faction asserts its superiority based on distinctive attributes, subjecting non-conforming fellow beings to servitude. The echoes of history resound, and we, as mere mortals, grapple with the legacies of ancient and recent prejudices.

Let's examine the concept of slavery, tracing its origins in societies like Ancient Mesopotamia and Ancient Egypt. In contrast to the more recent racialized enslavement of Africans, historical instances were often motivated by social, economic, or legal factors. Our investigation extends to antisemitism, charting its evolution from religious persecution in medieval times to the racialized form witnessed during the Nazi era.

Contemplating these historical injustices, we are confronted with the challenge of understanding prejudice and its connections to the human quest for control. Leaders throughout history—Alexander the Great, Julius Caesar, Emperor Qin Shi Huang, Napoleon Bonaparte, Adolf Hitler—are invoked as examples of ambition gone awry, causing destruction, committing mass murder, and ultimately returning to dust in the vast expanse of time.

Now, imagine a thought-provoking vision: What if these same leaders, instead of pursuing conquests, collaborated to address the collective challenges facing humanity? It highlights the continued struggle for authority, often at the expense of human suffering, even in contemporary society. The underlying theme suggests that prejudices, whether rooted in racism, religion, or any other form, often serve as a smokescreen for leaders driven by the desire to bend the world to their will.

The essence of this reflection lies in the recognition that as humanity progresses beyond its current state of underdeveloped civilization, the prevailing human tendency to harbor prejudices against others may gradually diminish. The discord here is that, contrary to what leaders may assert to the public, the primary motivation behind these prejudices often lies in the leaders' aspiration for global dominance. Whether it manifests through racism, religious bias, or any pretext justifying their actions, the underlying goal remains the same—to bend the world to their will.

However, a more optimistic perspective unfolds as societal evolution takes center stage. Over time, as we continue to advance, societies may witness a departure from the age-old pattern of leaders perpetuating suffering for their ambitions. This positive shift has indeed already occurred at various points in history, illustrating the potential for transformative leadership that influences the world in constructive ways. To achieve the ideal scenario in the quest for an evolved species, the ongoing journey and the resilience of humans to adhere to an elevated state of consciousness are pivotal.

## 25  THE INTRINSIC PURPOSE OF DEATH

In the state in which we find ourselves, endowed with limited understanding, the true meaning of death eludes our grasp. The mere mention of death on our planet invokes a panic that permeates the mind, encapsulating one of the greatest fears known to humanity. Considering this premise, have you ever paused to contemplate the paradox wherein we celebrate the birth of a human being but mourn their death? Some may argue it's due to the longing for the departed friend, yet, more often than not, it may be due to the way we perceive death as the ultimate end — an abyss of the unknown.

Consider, for a moment, a hypothetical scenario where knowledge reigns supreme: all humans, upon death, see their bodies return to the earth while their souls embark on a journey to another planet. In this alternate reality, the fear of death might diminish, and the prospect of suicide could become more prevalent, especially in the face of life's tribulations. The idea would be simple: if unhappiness prevails in this moment, why not choose to depart and join others in a different realm? It would seem almost too convenient, potentially leading many to abandon challenges rather than confront them.

Yet, this is precisely why the mystery of death remains veiled from humans. Without the certainty of what comes next, we are compelled to experience the progression of our lives on Earth, confronting challenges rather than prematurely ending our journey. The fear associated with death, often contemplated during moments of sadness, serves as a safeguard, preventing impulsive decisions. These controls and uncertainties are mechanisms designed to facilitate our existence on Earth, enabling us to undergo the full spectrum of evolutionary experiences before departing when the time is ripe — once the essential facets of life are fully developed.

The transition from birth to death is a meticulously orchestrated process. We arrive as infants, devoid of extensive knowledge, adapting to the intricacies of our planet. As we get old, our bodies and organs undergo a gradual decay, preparing us to detach from the material aspects of Earth. This process minimizes resistance as our souls depart.

Have you ever observed that numerous seniors convey a sense of having experienced a full life and being prepared for the next chapter? This is an acknowledgment of the exhaustion they've encountered in their earthly journey. A death occurring out of sync with the natural life cycle is often deemed a tragedy, as it disrupts the intended course. Conversely, we are more inclined to accept death as a natural part of existence when someone passes away due to old age.

Throughout history, various cultures and beliefs have shaped diverse perspectives on death. In the Viking era, death was viewed through the lens of an afterlife, where brave warriors found themselves in Valhalla. Hinduism regards death as a component of the cycle of reincarnation, with the soul undergoing rebirths until achieving liberation. The ancient Egyptians believed in an afterlife and practiced mummification for a successful journey.

Despite these disparate views, we must concede that death is as intrinsic to our existence as anything else on Earth. Building on our exploration in this book, where we've acknowledged the purpose in all creations and considered scientific principles like Aristotle's theory of cause and effect, we arrive at the commonsense conclusion that death serves a purpose. It plays an integral role in the grand scheme of our existence, regulating and balancing the number of living individuals at any given point in time. This mechanism, accounted for by nature's policing, ensures that we do not overpopulate Earth by living forever, thus guaranteeing the continual evolution of our species.

# 26  BREAKING FREE FROM SELF-IMPOSED PRISONS

At the core of our life's struggles lies one of the most significant contributors — our desires and wishes. While some argue that desires serve as mere motivators for conquest, the harsh reality is that they often spring from indulgence rather than genuine love. Consider the scenario where one dreams of a grand mansion with 25 rooms, equipped with all the opulence such a residence can offer. Initially, the fulfillment of this dream seems instantaneous, a sense of accomplishment coursing through every inch of the vast abode. Yet, as time unfolds, the mansion transforms from a symbol of triumph into a familiar dwelling. Most rooms remain unexplored, as the sheer size renders daily navigation impractical.

Eventually, routine sets in, with a few rooms becoming the sole focus — the kitchen, a specific bathroom, the garage, and perhaps one of the pools. Despite the mansion's expanse, the once-grand achievement dwindles into the equivalent of a one-bedroom apartment. This process repeats itself with other acquisitions, whether multiple cars or an abundance of clothing. Boredom creeps in as excess money accumulates, and other forms of necessities loom, such as extravagant travels to exotic locales.

As the allure of these pursuits fades over time, the realization emerges that something crucial may be missing, perhaps a meaningful relationship. This realization becomes even more apparent when embarking on a new relationship, where one envisions an ideal partner but encounters a fresh set of challenges. After two years, despite all the achievements, the perpetual question lingers – why isn't life consistently filled with happiness? Reflecting on the past, when possessions were scarce, the notion that hard work and the fulfillment of dreams would bring wealth and solve all problems prevailed. Yet, with wealth attained and dreams realized, a void persists.

Society perpetuates the belief that a peaceful and happy life aligns with monetary success. However, the disheartening reality contradicts this narrative, evident in the struggles of the wealthy or famous who succumb to despair. This predicament reflects a self-imposed prison, tethered to the notion that immense wealth guarantees peace and happiness. The truth, however, lies in cultivating a life filled with love, irrespective of material possessions.

At a crucial juncture in my life, I had an epiphany. I realized that an extensive amount of time had been dedicated to amassing wealth. One day, I took pause and spent a few hours gazing at the ocean. Believe me, I wasn't in a negative space, nor was I entertaining thoughts of ending this remarkable journey I had embarked on. But a revelation struck me — why was I perpetually in pursuit of wealth when moments of despair still lingered?

Departing from the beach that day, I intentionally chose to dispel the anxiety stemming from the relentless pursuit of fortune. Despite already being blessed beyond measure, I made a deliberate shift in focus, opting to pursue peace and happiness instead. The outcomes were unexpectedly transformative. I had never experienced a more profound sense of vitality. Possessions acquired in the pursuit of peace and happiness through wealth lost their significance. Enjoying an expensive asset or indulging in a luxurious experience became commonplace, no longer bound by an insatiable desire for indulgence.

The most remarkable part of this experience was that, by letting go, I eradicated the desire to navigate my daily life through the lens of acquired assets, maintaining a constant sense of accomplishment. Instead, peace and love came to me organically, without solicitation. My life transformed into something beautiful, and the clarity that emerged in work, business, family, and relationships was profound.

Throughout this journey, had I only realized that the key to my happiness lay in releasing the things that clung to it. This process involved shedding regrets, anger, desire, ego, and fear. Essential to this transformation was treating others with love, granting forgiveness for past grievances, and acknowledging that we are all susceptible to the same self-imposed prison. I firmly believe that this revelation stands as one of the most significant secrets to leading a fulfilled life. It merely necessitates the act of letting go, honing the mastery of higher vibrational energies, and eliminating all that obstructs our authentic selves.

# 27  JORDAN, JOBS, AND MUSK: LESSONS FROM TRUE BELIEVERS

In the realm of consciousness, many skeptics deny its creative power. Reflecting on our earlier discussions about the tangible nature of emotions, the substantiality of these energies is more palpable than commonly perceived. Some advocate the mantra that positive thinking begets positive outcomes, and while not entirely incorrect, those endorsing it often fall short of adhering to their own advice. You may find yourself wondering why some individuals seem to attract good fortune while others struggle. It's a question that naturally crosses our minds. The answer lies in the meticulous utilization of consciousness.

Recall our prior conversations on neutralizing negative energies in the workplace. Individuals emitting low vibrational energies impact those around them, evident in the conflicts experienced by multiple individuals. Awareness becomes crucial in discerning whether you might inadvertently be contributing to this energy dynamic. Let's explore a scenario where you are not the source of workplace discord.

You interact with a challenging individual daily, contemplating potential confrontations as a defense mechanism. The suffering extends beyond the workplace, as you unwittingly create a mental experience with this person that may never transpire. Unbeknownst to you, the mere act of thinking about them connects you with their energies more than you realize, exacerbating the situation. To regain control, one must master the art of conscious creation.

Consider the tale of Michael Jordan, cut from his high school basketball team during his sophomore year. Instead of accepting defeat, he returned home with a determination to prove himself in basketball. He transcended this setback, returning stronger and better. Some might attribute this to sheer determination, but is determination not steered by one's state of consciousness? His belief in envisioning greatness played a pivotal role, surpassing the significance of skill development through practice. This illustrates that, similarly, if you continually focus on life's hardships, viewing yourself as an unfortunate victim, you inadvertently create a reality that aligns with these negative thoughts, becoming the architect of your own defeat.

In 1989, Tim Berners-Lee identified the need for a more efficient way for researchers to share and retrieve information. Instead of keeping data in isolated systems, he envisioned a system that would enable people to easily connect and access information across different platforms. This vision laid the groundwork for what we now know as the World Wide Web. Similarly, at the pinnacle of his career, Steve Jobs achieved unparalleled success through visionary leadership at Apple, setting new standards for design aesthetics and user experience. His impact on both the PC and mobile sectors marked a pivotal moment in the evolution of personal computing and communication. Elon Musk has been a driving force in advancing space exploration and various other innovations. Many others who share an unrestricted consciousness have shifted and reshaped the way we live today, harnessing the boundless creative power within life's most potent tool.

The examples serve as illustrations, emphasizing that the life outcomes we manifest are a direct result of our conscious direction. If you embrace average thinking, you will live an average life. Dark thoughts will cast a shadow on your existence, while envisioning victory and channeling the power of creation will bring you triumph. Your mind is a potent tool for manifesting your desires, so guard your thoughts with the utmost care.

# 28  IS IT KARMA? EXPLORING THE COMMON GROUND OF CAUSE AND EFFECT

Most of us are familiar with the term "Karma," often invoked when we see someone facing consequences for their misdeeds. While commonly used to highlight retribution for wrongdoing, the concept of karma is far more intricate than our immediate perceptions might grasp. In our discussions about the scientific principles of cause and effect, we emphasized the importance of recognizing that events on Earth are not random occurrences but outcomes with antecedent causes. Ignoring these causal links would defy the fundamental laws of physics and the very essence of the universe.

Before delving into the concept of karma, let's explore diverse perspectives on the outcome of human existence. In Hinduism, for instance, there's a belief that one's actions in this life will reverberate in future lives—good deeds yielding positive consequences and vice versa. Christianity posits an afterlife where individuals face destinies in heaven or hell based on their faith in Jesus Christ. Judaism exhibits a variety of beliefs, from resurrection to concepts of paradise and purgatory, showcasing the rich diversity within different Jewish traditions.

Despite these variations, a common thread among these beliefs is the adherence to the concept of cause and effect. This reading aims not to challenge these beliefs but to encourage self-awareness beyond perceived limitations. Actions, when manifested, may be expressed through rights and wrongs throughout a lifetime—causes—and reactions materialize as the outcomes of these actions—effects. In essence, irrespective of different views and religious segregations, we universally agree on the principle that every action begets a reaction—a fundamental truth governing our universe.

Consider a person who leads a life marked by malevolence. Do we presume this individual to be exempt from justice? Conversely, someone dedicated to charitable deeds—does their goodness dissipate without consequence? If life were truly purposeless, a series of random occurrences without meaning, then why the need for senses like sight, hearing, speech, or even the act of breathing? Why aren't we just inert like a rock or a purposeless wax bubble? And even with limited perspectives, both play their part on Earth.

Estimates suggest that 108 to 115 billion inhabitants have traversed this Earth. If judgment is solely based on rights and wrongs with no room for redemption, is it equitable to condemn those from primitive times whose levels of consciousness were vastly different from ours today? Are individuals from historical periods, such as the era of the 18th-century slave trade, forever banished for acts that our contemporary consciousness condemns? If we consider human history, we observe the development of our understanding and consciousness. Though it may still pose challenges, our awareness has evolved from earlier times to our current state. Clearly, this progress is ongoing and will persist through the passage of time. Perhaps the concept of cause and effect plays a role in our souls, and redemption through afterlife trials, whether rebirth on Earth or elsewhere, awaits us, guided by forces beyond our current understanding.

# 29  PAST LIVES, PRESENT SKILLS: THE ENIGMA OF INHERITED ABILITIES

Back to the intriguing notion that some may consider humans as mere coincidences, devoid of any inherent purpose. Let's delve into our biological structure; contemporary science asserts that all humans share a fundamental similarity. While individual variations may exist, with some lacking certain body parts, the collective 7 billion inhabitants of our planet are essentially built with the same biological blueprint.

Now, if this uniformity is indeed accurate, how do we reconcile the evident disparities in skills among individuals? It's tempting to attribute these differences to mere practice, but the question lingers: if we are truly alike at a biological level, why do some grasp specific skills more swiftly than others? Consider this scenario: assemble 100 individuals to practice ballet with identical schedules, and you'll still witness varying levels of proficiency. Repeat the process with singing, and once again, certain individuals will outshine others. There's no guarantee that those excelling in ballet will replicate their success in singing.

Science often rushes to explain such phenomena through the lens of pre-existing factors and conditions, invoking the concept of genetic variations. This idea suggests that genetic diversity arises over time due to mutations, genetic recombination, and adaptations accumulated across generations. However, if we were to challenge this notion by considering the initial deployment of the first humans as all machines to be built equally, then we would agree that all humans would share the same capabilities, and divergences could not exist. At their inception, these early humans shared a common biological structure without the intricate genetic variations we understand today. Their genetic diversity was likely more limited compared to the extensive gene pool found in modern humans.

So, might their skills and abilities have been passed down genetically through time? It's a plausible theory. However, the unexpected display of exceptional singing prowess by a five-year-old challenges this conventional explanation. Moreover, siblings frequently showcase varying levels of wisdom, skills, and intelligence despite sharing genetic factors. This prompts us to consider the intriguing possibility that the mysteries of skill inheritance and development extend into uncharted territories—perhaps engraved in our very souls. Could they be remnants of past lives or derived from realms unknown to us? Only time will unveil these profound secrets.

One last enigma to ponder is the perplexing scenario where two siblings exhibit starkly incompatible behavioral traits despite sharing the same parents. While one child may display a calm, focused demeanor with an eagerness for personal development, the other might embrace a confrontational nature, gravitating towards erratic behaviors. Do we continue to attribute these disparities solely to genetic variations and predetermined factors, or could there be another unsolved mystery at play?

# 30 THE UNSPOKEN TRUTH BEHIND POVERTY

Why does poverty exist? Did you know that poverty wasn't meant to be the pervasive issue we're accustomed to, and it's not merely the inequality we're taught in classrooms and textbooks? Here's a truth seldom shared by those in power: "For a few to amass wealth, a majority must endure moderate poverty." This dynamic is crucial in any economy.

Consider inflation, a term citizens often hear about but may not fully understand. The government frames it as the rising cost of goods relative to earnings, fostering the belief that citizens can't afford basic necessities. In reality, a flourishing economy where everyone prospers is a utopian ideal, and there are two primary reasons for this.

Firstly, if everyone has substantial wealth, the prices of goods will rise to meet the increased demand, negating the initial prosperity. Secondly, who will undertake undesirable tasks if everyone can afford to delegate them? This scenario would create a new set of challenges, rendering wealth less meaningful.

Don't entertain the dream that every individual will enjoy wealth;

no economic system on this planet offers such a promise. Capitalism or socialism, neither provides an equitable distribution of wealth. This book doesn't aim to vilify any government but seeks to raise awareness. Leaders, like citizens, are fallible, and their allegiance to flawed systems perpetuates our collective struggles.

Our political system, celebrated for its democratic principles, often falters after elections, revealing an unsettling reality. Swapping administrations rarely leads to substantial change; we remain stuck in a cycle of unfulfilled promises. The blame lies not solely with our leaders but with each citizen unwilling to confront the need for personal and societal change.

The educational system neglects moral teachings while introducing divisive subjects like gender studies to young children. The pursuit of votes supersedes genuine progress. Initiatives that claim to improve society often exacerbate divisions rather than fostering unity.

True change starts from the bottom, from elevating our collective consciousness. Morality should be a cornerstone of education, guiding individuals toward a sense of responsibility for the greater good. Divisive strategies that pit us against each other must be replaced by a unified demand for what is right for the community, not just for individual gain.

The world is in disarray because we allow ourselves to be divided. Governments advocate for open borders and assistance to those in need while simultaneously engaging in conflicts that displace these very people. Collective elevation of consciousness is essential to eradicate evil and progress as an evolved species, taking strides towards a more compassionate and harmonious world.

# 31  BELLADONNA'S ANALOGY: THE REAP AND SOW EFFECT

Have you ever heard of Belladonna? Also known as Deadly Nightshade and scientifically labeled Atropa belladonna, it carries a mystique that stretches back to Greek mythology. Atropa, named after Atropos, the eldest of the Fates, the weaver of life's threads who, when the time came, cut them asunder.

The Fates – Clotho, Lachesis, and Atropos – held sway over humanity's destinies. While individuals retained free will, the Fates possessed knowledge of the ultimate choices and actions each would make. In the afterlife, judgment awaited based not solely on deeds but on how one grappled with life's tribulations.

Belladonna, a plant with potent and perilous properties, found its place in historical shadows. Despite potential medicinal and cosmetic applications, it played a role in witchcraft, clandestine plots, and, during the Roman Empire, shadowy political maneuvers. Agrippina the Younger, wife of Emperor Claudius, reportedly employed it on the counsel of Locusta, a reputed poison specialist, as did Livia, rumored to have used it in her husband Emperor Augustus's demise.

Shakespeare immortalized Belladonna in "Romeo and Juliet." In the poignant Act 5, Scene 3, the ill-fated lovers sealed their tragic end with a sequence of fatal events, culminating in a poison-laced kiss:

*'Arms, take your last embrace! And, lips, O you*
*The doors of breath, seal with a righteous kiss*
*A dateless bargain to engrossing death!*
*Come, bitter conduct, come, unsavory guide,*
*Here's to my love!*
*O true apothecary,*
*Thy drugs are quick. Thus with a kiss I die.'*

This echoes the biblical narrative of Adam and Eve, where the forbidden fruit – often referred to as the "fruit of the tree of the knowledge of good and evil" – set the stage for the laws of right and wrong, cause and effect. As the saying goes, "you reap what you sow," emphasizing the critical interplay between consciousness and action. In the saga of Adam and Eve, the conscious choice to partake in the forbidden fruit led to awareness, shame, and expulsion from the Garden of Eden. It's a reminder that our actions, consciously chosen, determine the harvest we reap.

Contemplate the creation of nuclear weapons. Though some may posit their development as a means of protection, their fundamental and exclusive function is the termination of lives. One cannot fire upon another and assert it was a medicinal intervention, an attempt to heal. Humanity pioneers the invention of nuclear weapons while anticipating global tranquility, a stance perpetually at odds with the principles of common sense.

The analogy of Belladonna serves as a stark reminder: planting certain seeds in life inevitably yields a corresponding harvest. Whether it's the acts of star-crossed lovers, the machinations of historical figures, or the choices in the biblical narrative, the fruit originating from the act shapes the trajectory of human existence. "Reap and sow" is tied to the laws of cause and effect, underlying the principle of crafting humanity's paths, determining whether we will endure more suffering or embrace salvation. This concept is crucial to one's existence as it defines one's life outcome, collectively driving the outcome of our world. Everything we do on this planet is a construction of our actions—a concept that might be easier for some to understand than others, but it's the ultimate legacy of our destinies.

## 32  LIFE LESSONS FROM THE DIVINE GOD, BRUCE ALMIGHTY

Why is it such a challenge for us to shape our lives according to our desires, precisely when we desire them? We have this tendency to always want more,

In our relentless pursuit of desires, we metaphorically resemble infants in the vast cosmos, exhibiting emotional struggles that contribute to considerable suffering—similar to a child's distress in persuading a parent to acquire a coveted item. This metaphor highlights the intricate nature of human desires, reflecting the complexities of our existence.

To delve deeper into this concept, let us turn our attention to the cinematic lens of "Bruce Almighty." Within this narrative, Jim Carrey's character, Bruce Nolan, is bestowed divine powers by God. As Bruce undertakes the arduous task of responding to prayers and fulfilling the wishes of all individuals, chaos erupts, and pandemonium ensues, serving as a fictional representation that delves further into the intricacies of human desires.

Surveying the world in which we presently reside, we witness leaders engaging in reckless and juvenile conquests, disrupting cities and lives without regard for humanity beyond their personal acquisitions. Simultaneously, we observe a societal shift where individuals are increasingly driven by the pursuit of wealth and fame, often at the expense of deeper values. Consider, for a moment, what would transpire if we were to grant every human desire and wish. In such a scenario, one that we may instinctively recoil from, I posit that the continued existence of our world would be tenuous at best, lasting perhaps not more than a week, given the unchecked nature of these dreams.

Hence, we encounter the purpose behind the trials and tribulations that shape the human experience, a process that allows us to earn credit when it is rightfully due. This may not always be immediately apparent, but through the lens of time and reflection, we come to understand the significance of these experiences.

The underlying message emphasizes that certain aspects of life can only be comprehended through the lens of maturity, aligning with the laws of the universe. It cautions against conflating enlightenment with the accumulation of worldly wealth, among other things, and underscores that genuine maturity unfolds as a profoundly spiritual journey. As individuals ascend to higher levels of understanding, the intricacies of life become clearer, revealing insights into purpose, mission, and the pursuit of the peace, happiness, and love destined for us to attain.

# 33  UNDERSTANDING THE LAWS OF TRANSFORMATION

In the earlier sections of this book, we explored the impact of natural elements like winds and oceans on our lives. Now, let's shift our focus to the profound consequences when these elements spiral out of control, resulting in hurricanes, earthquakes, and other disruptive events. While human neglect is undeniably a contributing factor, the second root cause is deeply embedded in the natural order — the fundamental principle of transformation.

Transformation, a ubiquitous force governing the universe, is not a mere process but a law that shapes the destiny of celestial bodies. Consider Earth's history, marked by ice ages, the rise and fall of dominant species, and the extinction of various life forms. Charles Darwin's theory of evolution by natural selection aligns with this ongoing process, emphasizing the shared ancestry of all living beings and their gradual adaptation over time.

Accepting Darwin's proposition leads us to the realization that transformation is a natural law, directed by the inherent forces of nature. It determines the fate of species, regulating what thrives, what diminishes, and what undergoes metamorphosis. The question of who governs this cosmic law remains elusive, perhaps beyond our comprehension given our earthly perspective.

Yet, what matters is the recurring demonstration that transformation is not just an ideal state but a necessity for evolution. Whether we embrace it willingly or resist its influence, we find ourselves compelled to comply with this universal law. So, when life seems complex, expectations falter, and feelings of anxiety or uncertainty prevail, remember a guiding principle — the laws of transformation.

The disruptions in your life act as signals for change. Are you overindulging, struggling with substance abuse, or constantly battling anger? Life's challenges exert a force commensurate with your inner strength, urging you to transform and ascend into a higher state of consciousness. Embracing this process leads to personal advancement and the acquisition of knowledge, paving the way for triumph.

As we navigate the dynamics of transformation, let us acknowledge its role in our lives and recognize that adaptation and changes are integral to our journey. In understanding and harnessing the essence of transformation, we find the keys to unlocking our truest selves.

There is an intriguing factor ingrained in our souls, a force that we sometimes grapple with—the innate push towards balance. Reflecting on our earlier discussion of gravitational forces, the stability of our solar system relies on the gravitational interactions between the Sun and various celestial bodies, including planets, moons, and other objects. Interestingly, our lives share a similar essence.

Consider the abuse of a drug. Each instance of consumption

triggers the addiction factor, driven by our body's chemical transformation, compelling us to seek more. Often, a hidden motive lurks in our subconscious. This echoes the principles of "reap and sow" and "cause and effect." The aftermath, the withdrawal effect, exacts a negative reaction commensurate with what was consumed. These adverse effects can manifest in physical discomfort, cognitive impairment, emotional distress, and other health-related issues.

Amidst these negative reactions, a subconscious question arises: "When will this finally end? I can't keep going like this." This internal inquiry parallels the gravitational force pushing us toward balance. Whether we embrace it or not, our existence is governed by this illustrative gravitational force.

Just as celestial bodies evolve, so do we. Balancing and evolution are intrinsic, woven into our being, much like the inseparable connection between our brain and body. They are integral parts of who we are.

# 34  TWO TRILLION IN GLOBAL MILITARY EXPENDITURES

In the grand tapestry of technological history, 1983 emerges as a watershed year with the introduction of the Motorola DynaTAC 8000X, affectionately known as the "brick phone" for its substantial size and weight. This pioneering device marked a seismic shift from car phones to the handheld, portable marvels that now define our communication landscape.

Over four decades, the mobile technology industry has undergone a remarkable transformation, evolving from rudimentary pioneering mobile handset contraptions to sophisticated handheld computers boasting operating systems, expansive storage, and a myriad of industrial and social functionalities. This rapid progress owes much to the cultural drive from advanced nations, where modest ideas transmute into monumental innovations.

Year after year, the United States has played a pivotal role in reshaping technology and other industries, birthing newer, better, and more sophisticated iterations. This dynamism isn't confined to technology alone, as seen in the Starbucks phenomenon. Starting as a humble coffee shop in 1971, Starbucks, then under Howard Schultz's stewardship, transformed into a revenue powerhouse, reaching $10.2 million in 1988 and now boasting a valuation of $105 billion. A similar spirit of innovation pulsates through Apple Inc., a technological giant approaching a staggering $3 trillion valuation.

Contemplating the historic 1969 moon landing, where primitive technology televised live images of men on the moon, prompts contemplation about our current challenges in justifying space exploration with technology a hundredfold more advanced. Despite the quantum leaps in consumer technology, space exploration seems to lag behind, prompting introspection on the evolution of our priorities.

A brief detour to the Washington, D.C. UFO incident of 1952 sparks speculation. Radar detections and visual observations fueled sightings, and despite compelling pilot testimonies, the U.S. Air Force dismissed these encounters as radar anomalies and misidentifications. Project Blue Book, established in 1952 to investigate UFO reports, concluded in 1969—the same year the United States launched men to the moon, marking a milestone in the space race with the USSR during the Cold War.

As the calendar flips to late 2023, UFO sightings once again seize the public imagination, thrusting mysterious extraterrestrial phenomena back into the limelight. Against this backdrop, a fresh cold war looms on the horizon, casting shadows of geopolitical tension. Surprisingly, collaborative initiatives aimed at reshaping our evolution appear notably absent from the list of global priorities. The historical perspective paints a puzzling picture: the iconic launches of Project Blue Book, Sputnik 1, NASA's inception, and the monumental Moon landing were all catalyzed by a Space Race, an emblematic manifestation of Cold War dynamics that ignited a new epoch of political, military, technological, and scientific prowess.

Despite recent technological advancements and staggering financial resources, nearly 200 billion dollars have been squandered in the destructive wake of conflicts orchestrated by a handful of leaders. Meanwhile, NASA allocates funds to Space X in a collaborative effort to reach the moon. The paradox emerges: we possess advanced technology, substantial funds for lunar exploration, yet the infrastructure remains stagnant since the historic achievement of 1969. Something, it seems, doesn't quite add up.

As the paradox deepens, budgetary disputes over space programs, such as the intricate saga surrounding the James Webb Space Telescope, only serve to accentuate the disconcerting dissonance within our global priorities. This stark contrast, where wars receive seemingly boundless financial support, while essential space exploration initiatives face intricate debates, raises profound questions about the trajectory of our collective journey. Worldwide military expenditures have soared to 2.24 trillion dollars, while funding for space exploration lingers at a mere 400 billion dollars. It prompts reflection on the allocation of resources – vast amounts invested in military capabilities to protect ourselves, but from whom exactly? Each other?

The spotlight on these conflicting priorities not only exposes hesitancy to invest in collaborative space exploration but also prompts reflection on the broader implications for the evolution of our species. At this puzzling crossroads, the drive toward destructive tendencies appears to outweigh the momentum needed for unified efforts toward collective growth.

Even as budgetary disputes over space programs, such as the James Webb Space Telescope, clash with ample funding allocated to wars, our priorities reveal a reluctance to invest in collaborative space exploration, impeding our species' evolution. The stark contrast becomes even more apparent when contemplating the superior capabilities of our modern mobile phones versus our delay in landing on the moon over five decades later, raising a perplexing question: why does our evolution seem to be delayed by a hundredfold?

# 35  FACES BEHIND SCREENS: A SOCIAL MEDIA DILEMMA

In a preceding segment, we underscored the importance of embracing a 24-hour intermission from our incessant thoughts. Our generation confronts an imposing challenge in the domain of mental health. With the relentless march of technology and the dawn of social media, our social experiences have undergone a profound transformation. The voices, faces and gestures of our friends and family, once physically present, are now virtualized through a handheld device.

While some may argue that they are in constant touch with loved ones, the reality is that interactions often occur solely through a mobile screen, and they may not have seen a family member or a friend in person for an entire year or longer. Even those they communicate with daily may struggle to recall the last face-to-face moment shared. Despite the illusion of constant connection, virtual interactions frequently overshadow physical presence.

It's alarming that we live in a world where our day-to-day

companion, the one we can't imagine living without, is most likely our mobile phone. The panic that ensues when someone loses their phone in today's society underscores the extent of this issue. It often goes largely unnoticed; our perception tricks us into believing we are surrounded by people and meaningful relationships, fostering the illusion of a highly social world. However, the reality portrays a much distinct picture – we spend our days clutching a mobile device and can't seem to restrain ourselves from doing so.

Imagine recording your behavior over 24 hours, then watching it back. The perspective might surprise you, providing a whole other view of what your life really looks like and revealing a reality many of us fail to recognize — the increasing loneliness of human beings. Unbeknownst to us, this isolation can lead to a cascade of mental health issues, with many unaware of their origin.

To fill this emptiness, there emerges an urge to showcase an entire life experience on social media. Unwittingly, we seek to overcome this void by creatively constructing unrealistic scenarios for others to perceive our completeness. However, the harsh truth is that this pursuit lacks genuine fulfillment. If it were otherwise, our primary focus would be immersing ourselves in the actual experience, rather than meticulously curating a succession of preliminary snapshot drafts to determine the best fit. "Inventing Anna," played by Julia Garner in the Netflix series, portrays how far a person would go to reinvent reality.

Many of us fall into the trap of turning our lives into virtual realities, resembling reality shows where little authenticity is conveyed. Consider how often you check your phone after posting a story. Despite convincing yourself that the number of views isn't a factor, the desire to know persists. You find yourself constantly checking for likes, comments, and new followers.

This obsession extends to the choices you make in your life. Your selection of a restaurant or outfit becomes driven not only by the experience itself but also by how it will look in a snapshot or footage. Unwittingly, you transform into a celebrity of an app, believing you stand out among others. The intentionally provided options to label yourself as a "Public Person" or adorn a blue ribbon on Instagram are designed to influence, encouraging a false sense of accomplishment. The very companies that design these apps gather enough data to assess user behavior. Working with a team of human behavioral specialists, psychologists, among others, they ensure the app is updated accordingly. App designers do this not only to serve the best usability but also to imperatively prioritize user retention at all costs, ultimately fostering user addiction.

Arriving at a rooftop restaurant in Los Angeles, I handed my car to the valet, only to encounter an intriguing spectacle. Five young women, each accompanied by a photographer, captured the attention of onlookers with a flurry of snapshots. Despite the apparent glamour, a peculiar realization struck me – those at the entrance seemed oblivious to the identity of these women. Fueled by curiosity, I approached one of the photographers and inquired, "Who are they?" With a hint of mockery, he responded, "Instagram Models." Further probing led to an unexpected revelation: these were not paparazzi but freelancers hired by the influencers themselves. Their task was to craft an illusion of celebrity status, ensuring that the world beyond the lens remained ignorant of their true identities. The photographer, with a certain swagger, affirmed, "That's why nobody here knows their identities." Intrigued, I discovered their profiles, boasting millions of followers. Yet, anonymity persisted among the passersby, prompting a realization of the profound lengths people go for social media fame. Even though these individuals were famous on social media, their fame didn't translate into recognition or awareness among people in the real-world setting. This encounter underscored the captivating power of social media, leaving me astounded at how these platforms enthrall users, making them unwittingly crave the allure of online recognition, even if the returns grant no added value.

Social media companies excel at getting users addicted to their platforms, leading to unfortunate consequences such as fatal accidents resulting from risky snapshots, dangerous challenges, and cyberbullying. Observing the time consumed in crafting stories and posts on social media reveals that the majority adds little value. Content gaining engagement is subject to the platform's discretion, often guided by policies that prioritize company sales while neglecting moderation on the intense display of sexuality.

The damages inflicted by social media platforms on people's lives are seldom at the center of discussions. Negative aspects remain obscured from public view. It's not a call to abandon these applications, but rather a plea to acknowledge the responsibilities associated with the damages they cause in our social lives. Efforts to address online safety and mental health awareness, particularly among the youth, are insufficient. The reality is that we are all affected to varying degrees without fully realizing the depth of our entanglement. To test your dependence, try abstaining from any social media app for 24 hours. If you find it challenging, you likely belong to the higher percentage mentally affected by it.

# 36  DRUG ESCAPES: FROM TEMPORARY RELIEF TO FULFILLED CONSCIOUSNESS

In our exploration of diverse topics, my intention has been to encourage you to contemplate life from a different perspective. It's an acknowledgment that we are not beings fully developed as we might presume, with uncharted realms within our souls waiting to be unlocked. This unlocking is the pathway to achieving the ultimate divine power, a state brimming with peace, love, and happiness.

The challenge arises when life is perceived as a race against time, fueled by the fear that opportunities will elude us, and the ticking clock leads us inevitably towards death. The daily trials, often not fully understood, contribute to a collective burden, injecting doses of anxiety into our lives. The pressing question remains: "How do we achieve a fulfilling life when it appears that everything is working against us?"

Let's embark on this exploration by embracing foundational concepts before delving into the pursuit of the ultimate entry to divinity. Consider the motivations behind the consumption of alcohol and recreational drugs. These substances provide a sense of liberation from our current conscious states. Not advocating for complete obliteration, as that leads to intoxication, but emphasizing their passive use for illustrative purposes.

Individuals tend to seek these substances as a momentary relief from the entrapments of traumas persistently buried in our subconscious. Some turn to alcohol and drugs for a fleeting sense of happiness or euphoria, while others seek escape from problems or moments of sorrow. However, the traumas persist, resurfacing once awareness returns to our day-to-day lives.

This aspect of our lives demands careful attention. The struggles of releasing these subconscious traumas often lead to addictions—a temporary break from life's challenges.

Recently, individuals grappling with traumas, anxieties, and depression have explored Ayahuasca ceremonies. Originating from South American Indigenous cultures in the Amazon and Orinoco basins, this psychoactive brew has evolved into urban centers in North America and Europe. It shows therapeutic potential in treating substance dependence, anxiety, and mood disorders.

Ayahuasca ceremonies typically involves the consumption of the Ayahuasca psychoactive brew, which is made from a combination of plants, most notably Banisteriopsis caapi and Psychotria viridis. The active ingredient responsible for its psychoactive effects is DMT (dimethyltryptamine), a powerful hallucinogenic compound.

Ayahuasca ceremonies, often led by experienced shamans or spiritual guides familiar with the traditional and spiritual use of Ayahuasca, aim to open a doorway to the spiritual realm, offering participants profound insights, self-discovery, and healing experiences. Commonly reported effects include vivid hallucinations, intense introspection, emotional release, and a sense of connection with the spiritual or natural world. The experience is frequently described as both challenging and transformative, with the potential to address deep-seated emotional issues, traumas, and psychological struggles.

It's crucial to note that certain participants in Ayahuasca ceremonies have reported instances of challenging or "bad trips," which may open doors to darker experiences during the process. Without advocating for or against the healing methods and benefits that these experiences may or may not provide, it's important to stress that the use of drugs and brews as ways to attain peace and happiness may come at a cost. While some herbs have been found medicinal to alleviate the burdens of our planet, others may cause more damage than one may anticipate. This underscores the importance of emphasizing soul healing through the pursuit of elevated consciousness. Such intentional and gradual soul evolution is essential, steering clear of shortcuts that may not necessarily align with the depth of soul transformation one seeks.

These examples underscore where the root of our life's problems resides—in our subconscious. By cultivating a supreme consciousness and elevating our awareness, we can permanently release these traumas, fulfilling the true purpose of our existence. It might initially sound absurd, especially for those deeply wounded, but managing these traumas is essential.

Anger, frustration, and stress, embedded in our subconscious, grow exponentially with each uncontrollable manifestation in our day-to-day trials, plunging individuals deeper into despair. Many remain oblivious to this process, unwittingly steering themselves towards depression and thoughts of suicide. Such processes also contribute to the development of psychological behaviors that may culminate in individuals turning into serial killers or murderers, among other disturbing outcomes. The key is to persistently navigate towards the right direction, no matter how daunting it may seem initially.

Trust in this process guarantees emergence from any situation into a more fulfilling life. It marks the true awakening of your consciousness, guiding you towards a divine stance for your soul. It's then that life and everything around you begin to make more profound sense. Our next discussion will explore practical ways to enhance this inherent power within you.

# 37  WHY ARE WE HERE ON EARTH? EXPLORING THE TRUE MEANING OF LIFE

Let us delve into a fundamental inquiry that has intrigued humanity for ages: What is our purpose on Earth? The answer, though seemingly straightforward, carries profound weight—our journey toward soul enlightenment. To put this to the test, consider a simple challenge: ask anyone to go through a whole day without a single negative action or thought. It's likely to be quite a task.

Imagine trying to avoid feelings of shame, guilt, anger, desire, pride, hate, or sadness for just one day. Even in mundane situations like waiting for breakfast, it's a significant challenge. Personally, as I waited for my morning meal, a negative thought slipped in: "I'm so hungry; this guy is taking too long." This momentary lapse revealed impatience and triggered a slight anxiety—a glimpse into the constant flow of thoughts we face every day.

Returning to a key theme in this book, let's consider the laws of cause and effect—a principle deeply embedded in the fabric of the universe. This principle highlights the importance of our thoughts and actions, emphasizing the power of mindful creation.

Take a practical example: your partner, in a rush, leaves a wet towel on the bed. Later, you find it. Now, you face a choice—do you calmly pick up the towel, or do you get angry and harbor resentment? Here, two events occur: the partner's action of leaving the wet towel and your reaction to it—two causes likely to lead to different effects.

Now, let's envision the potential progression of this narrative. You decide to communicate with your partner, sending a message like, "Honey, you left the wet towel in bed." Your partner responds with, "Sorry, I was in a rush; could you please put it away? I'll be more careful next time." In this scenario, both individuals approach the situation consciously, sidestepping a day overshadowed by conflict over a simple towel. Such deliberate behavior signifies a step toward personal evolution.

On the contrary, the second outcome could unfold as a blame game. "Am I supposed to pick up a wet towel for you?" retorts the partner, "What are you complaining about? You forgot to lock the door; it was open when I left this morning." This turns into a contest of blame, akin to two nations on the brink of declaring war. Both reactions leave the individuals in a state of uneven consciousness, demanding future reconciliation. Often, these manifestations of underdeveloped consciousness act as catalysts for relationship breakdowns.

At this point, you may question the practicality of these ideals in real-life situations. The truth is, putting them into practice is far more challenging than describing them. Undoubtedly, this encapsulates the essence of the entire book—a formidable yet transformative journey. Just as mastering the violin necessitates practice, achieving mastery over consciousness calls for persistent effort. The predicament lies in the fact that many are unaware of the necessity of such mastery.

Governments, schools, parents—entities wielding significant influence—rarely underscore the importance of this journey, exemplifying our species' considerable lag in evolution.

Consider recent efforts by governments to incorporate discussions on gender and identity matters into school programs. Interestingly, as adults, we grapple with these issues, yet we contemplate introducing them to our schools. The very leaders guiding us on this Earth are the architects of our future, emphasizing the precarious nature of our current situation.

Revisiting the theme of mastering consciousness, a concrete instrument brimming with potential to shape the course of our lives, it becomes imperative to recognize the pivotal role that morality, well-being, love, and other elevated states of consciousness play in our salvation. A pressing question demands our attention—why do these vital subjects not occupy a central position in our educational programs? While we diligently impart knowledge of scientific disciplines to navigate the intricate web of societal structures, we tend to overlook essential subjects that nurture our moral and spiritual development.

In the contemporary world, a pervasive absence of love and companionship is glaringly evident. Individualism holds sway, divorce rates skyrocket, and relationships become increasingly transient. This societal unrest stems from our relentless pursuit of material concerns, a pursuit that often leaves the profound values of peace, love, and happiness grievously neglected.

Contemplate the analogy of bringing home a dog displaying anger, biting, and incessant barking. The necessity for a pet trainer becomes evident to eliminate these instinct-driven, low-vibrational behaviors. Dogs, immersed in emotional realms, serve as a testament to the transformative influence of emotional understanding. The pet owner bears witness to the transformation of an initially irate dog into a loving companion. Dogs, unlike humans, don't attend school to learn capitalistic ideals; their education centers around matters of emotion.

Ponder the wisdom encapsulated in the saying, "The more I learn about people, the more I love my dog." Have we ever contemplated why this statement resonates so profoundly? It signifies a genuine yearning for unconditional love within the human experience. Elevating our consciousness to evolve into beings of love is imperative for the advancement of our species, ultimately leading to the eradication of suffering—where hatred, killing, ego, greed, and other manifestations of malevolence cease to exist.

Imagine an improbable scenario: five dogs conspiring to rob a bank. If such a tale were true, it would undoubtedly captivate the world's attention, constituting a profound anomaly—akin to the sudden arrival of aliens on Earth. It would be a revolutionary shock to the world. Yet, isn't our human behavior equally anomalous? We routinely engage in actions that, when objectively observed, appear absurd. Our collective indifference to this absurdity underscores the blind spots within our societal consciousness.

Without delving into the intricacies of politics and recognizing that individuals' actions often stem from external influences, it's essential to underscore that the driving force behind these actions remains consciousness. People seek wealth not due to inherent poverty but are spurred by the observation of others' affluence. Desires, fueled by a low vibrational level of consciousness, perpetuate societal patterns.

So, how do we free ourselves from this quagmire when a significant portion of humanity resides within these low vibrational states of consciousness? The journey begins with self-reflection and self-control. Recognize and manage the moments when negative thoughts attempt to infiltrate your mind. Consider adopting a protective mantra for potential discord, such as: "I acknowledge the limitations, as I am committed to keeping my consciousness unburdened and elevated." Feel free to create your own mantra to protect yourself when actions or thoughts, whether from others or yourself, attempt to unbalance your conscious states. The transformative impact of such a practice is profound.

When friends and family inquire, "How do you manage to stay happy all the time?" my response remains constant, "I shield my states of elevated consciousness from any burden attempting to sway them, no matter how challenging or profound the circumstances may seem." The path to consciousness mastery is undeniably challenging, but the rewards are life-altering. It necessitates a commitment to self-awareness, a commitment to becoming architects of our own happiness, and a commitment to evolving beyond the limitations that hold us back. As we embark on this journey, let us collectively strive for a higher plane of consciousness, contributing to the collective elevation of humanity.

# 38  PATHS TO PEACE: SEEKING ONE GOD IN DIVERSE TRADITIONS

In exploring the relationships between different belief systems, our focus is not on idealism or the challenges each presents, as that goes beyond the reading's purpose. Instead, we delve into the notion that, despite the diversity of groups on Earth, our limited consciousness obstructs us from fully grasping the knowledge of the universe. Despite the segregation, freewill allows us to seek similar doctrines.

Without claiming priority or disputing diverse opinions, let's explore various entities in different religions:

Christianity: Jesus Christ
Islam: Allah (God)
Judaism: Yahweh (God)
Buddhism: Siddhartha Gautama (Buddha)
Hinduism: Various deities including Brahma, Vishnu, Shiva
Umbanda: Various spiritual beings
Shintoism: Kami (Spiritual beings)
Bahá'í Faith: Bahá'u'lláh (Founder)

Sikhism: Waheguru (God)
Jainism: Tirthankaras (Enlightened beings)
Zoroastrianism: Ahura Mazda (Supreme God)

A common thread emerges among major world religions—they often share a foundational belief in a higher power or adored figure, guided by teachings or scriptures. Despite variations in expressions, rituals, and doctrines, the core concept of a divine being is a universal element.

This shared template often includes principles of morality, ethical conduct, and a framework for understanding life's purpose and meaning. Despite diversity, there's a universal human inclination to seek answers to profound questions, giving rise to various religions united by a common pursuit of the divine.

In ancient times, our pursuit of enlightenment shared a similar foundation:

Greek Mythology: Zeus, Poseidon, Hera, Athena, Apollo, others
Roman Religion: Jupiter, Juno, Venus, Mars, others
Norse Religion (Vikings): Odin, Loki, Thor, Freyja, others
Ancient Egyptian Religion: Ra, Isis, Anubis, Osiris, others
Ancient Mesopotamian Religion: Inanna, Anu, Enlil, others

Across different eras, humans have consistently adhered to fundamental principles, even when their beliefs slightly diverged due to distinctions discussed earlier. A comparative analysis of modern and ancient religions reveals a remarkable evolution in human consciousness. While violence persists on Earth, significant progress has been made compared to the beliefs of earlier eras.

In the contemporary world, there is a heightened emphasis on diplomacy, negotiation, and international cooperation to address conflicts and global challenges. The existence of powerful military technologies, coupled with a profound awareness of the catastrophic consequences of large-scale conflicts, has motivated nations to prioritize diplomatic solutions. Despite this progress, the acknowledgment remains that we are an underdeveloped species in the eyes of the universe.

The question arises: Will we willingly subject ourselves to further challenging times to facilitate additional progression? The likelihood is high, and with each instance, we are poised to evolve through newer phases, contributing to the ongoing evolution of our souls during our journeys on this Earth.

www.ingramcontent.com/pod-product-compliance
Lightning Source LLC
Chambersburg PA
CBHW052042150726
48002CB00002B/714